THE TECHNICOLOR COMMUNITY

OR

THE TEKNIKOLOR KINGDOM:

REALIZING THE DREAM OF
MULTICULTURAL CONGREGATIONS

Dr. Carl V. Johnson

PRESS

FORWARD

The story of thirty years of ministry in a local church is rare in any location or culture today. The life of Gracepoint Gospel Fellowship is an extraordinary testimony to God's amazing power to change lives and blend people in ministry and community beyond predictable boundaries.

This book documents the breaking down of barriers and building together of the Kingdom of God. Congregations don't drift in this multicultural expression without grace and love being experienced in extraordinary measure. God's heart for all the nations of the world is the intention revealed from Genesis to Revelation. God's promise to Abraham was worldwide in scope. The end of history revealed in the Book of Revelation includes a vision of people from every language, tribe and nation declaring the praise of God assembled around the throne.

This reality was the celebration recorded in Acts 16 when the new congregation assembled in Philippi included a woman, a slave and a Gentile as well as the Apostle Paul, a recovering Jewish Pharisee. The power of the Gospel breaks down barriers and builds supernatural bridges of new relationship. Each believer has more in common with another believer than any former associations of family, race, language or color. Now adopted into the same family all can rejoice to call each other brother and sister through faith in Christ.

My own experience of membership in a Latino church fellowship for nine years confirmed the manifold grace of God in a culturally diverse church. I learned new lessons from my brothers and sisters about love, community, prayer and the power of the Gospel to change lives. Issues of justice for the poor and practical action marked our life together. Through an educational partnership students were tutored, mentored and prepared for college education. Everybody received more than they ever dreamed possible in relationships designed to build each other up into the best possible people we could be.

The research that Carl Johnson has documented in this book only demonstrates what Jesus said in John 13:34,35 " A new commandment I give you: Love one another. As I have loved you, so you must love one another. By this all men will know that you are my disciples, if you love one another." Gracepoint Gospel Fellowship gets the Gospel right and their life together has been a radical expression in New City and the region where they have had such a powerful impact.

This book will serve as an invitation to other individuals and churches to practice this radical Gospel of love in community without barriers. To those on the journey rejoice, for you have a watching world that still needs to see and know the reality of true discipleship as we love one another.

Dr. David Midwood
Former President Vision New England

INTRODUCTION

T his book has grown out of my experience pastoring the same church for thirty plus years. Little did my wife and I know when we came to New City, NY in 1977 that we would spend our lives shepherding the same congregation. The church, in this northern suburb of NYC, has gone from a completely homogeneous, or as some would term it, a "lily white" congregation, to being one of the most diverse congregations in America. Today the congregation at Gracepoint Gospel Fellowship (formerly New City Gospel Fellowship) is composed of approximately equal numbers of Blacks, Whites and Hispanics along with a smaller but significant Asian population. Research done in 1990, by George Barna, Christian researcher par excellence, showed that seventy-nine percent of churches in America were homogeneous – that is made up of just one racial or ethnic group. Eighteen percent of churches were "borderline" (having a minority population of 1 to 10%) and only three percent of congregations in this country were classified "multicultural" (meeting a minimal standard of eleven percent minority). Unfortunately, to my knowledge, more recent reliable data is not available.

As I have described the composition of our church to other pastors and church leaders I was invariably asked the question, "How did that happen?" I was not really certain exactly how or why this rare occurrence had taken place in suburban New York. I speculated about certain characteristics of our church, about myself, the staff, the congregation, the worship style, etc. but I had no solid answers. In 2006 I began a doctoral project where the purpose was "to identify and to understand factors that lead minorities to attend and assimilate into a multicultural congregation or a congregation made up primarily of another ethnicity, rather than remaining in or joining a church of their own race or ethnicity." The hypothesis to be tested was that there are certain key identifiable elements of a congregation (and its leadership) that attract and draw racial or ethnic minority individuals. I really hoped to come up with some answers, for myself and for others; answers that might assist those who are longing to see the development of multicultural congregations. I continue to meet more and more pastors who are committed to seeing this ideal realized in their own settings.

The stated objective of my project was "to identify these elements for subsequent implementation by other churches in creating a more effective outreach to multicultural communities." Ultimately, the importance of the project was based on the supposition that such a multiracial, multiethnic congregation could be a potent witness of the unity that believers enjoy in Christ as well as a witness of the power of the gospel to break down societal barriers. The desired outcome could be the restoration or incorporation of people for whom the failure of the church to address racial issues has been such a dark blot.

This book follows the general format required for my Doctor of Ministry project although I have attempted to make it less technical for the lay reader. The first chapter is the Biblical-theological foundation for understanding diversity and reconciliation as key components of God's plan for the ages and for the church of Jesus Christ. Although the Black church has historically been very concerned with the issue of justice due to the Black experience in America, white pastors and congregations seldom address the issues of diversity, justice, discrimination and reconciliation of races. I have sought to demonstrate that these issues are central to God's concerns and that in the Bible, from cover to cover, we find the heart of God inclined toward the nations.

The second chapter reviews literature and opinions dealing with the multicultural church and issues of diversity. The controversy between advocates of the homogeneous unit principle (HUP), found in church growth material, and those who strongly oppose this principle on Biblical grounds is presented. Questions addressed are: Can multicultural churches flourish? What are the unifying factors? Should multicultural churches be encouraged? What are the benefits of multicultural churches? How intentional must the church be in all this? How do we prepare a local church for cultural diversity? And finally, how do we understand and minister to other cultures?

A qualitative case study involving members of Gracepoint Gospel Fellowship (GGF), an extremely integrated, multicultural congregation, was used to identify factors that led minorities to attend this church and, in most cases, to leave a church of their own race or ethnicity. A broad survey, responded to by over two hundred attendees, as well as a subsequent open-ended questionnaire given to a select group of minority attendees, was developed. The survey and questionnaire focused on barriers that a minority person faces and overcomes in attending a majority or multicultural congregation as well as factors that might attract a minority individual to such a church. The data collected from these surveys was analyzed using a methodology known as Concept Mapping.

A similar study focusing on multicultural churches was carried out by George Yancey in 2003. His study employed feedback from pastors and church leaders whereas I asked congregants to share their personal reasons for moving from an ethnic church to a white or multicultural church. I then took the list of reasons they supplied and had them rank them to determine which issues they felt were of greatest concern. I believe that there were clear advantages in this approach. I am satisfied that, at the end of this research, the people have spoken. I believe that the results are simple to comprehend and embrace. Sometimes simple is good.

DEDICATION AND ACKNOWLEDGEMENTS

(C S)

I dedicate this project to my partner in ministry and companion in love and life, Diana Sherice (always Sherry to me and now Dr. Johnson, yes even to me). She has stood by me through thick and thin. She has labored by my side and so often behind the scenes, not seeking attention or credit, but seeking to bless the lives of others in quiet but very effective ways. She is forever the counselor, deeply gifted in discerning the hearts and feelings of others, and offering wisdom and understanding. She has so often blessed my own life with her sense of intuition and her perceptive nature. I would also like to acknowledge my children, Nathan, Daniel and Kara for their love and their faithfulness to the Lord and the joy that they have consistently brought to my life. Along with them I am thankful for the two daughters added "along the way," Sadie and Irisha, who have certainly added to the blessing and happiness of my life. Finally, I can only say that the joy of living has been multiplied with the addition of five grandchildren, Samantha, Daniel, Elijah <u>Carl</u>, Azlan and Kaiel. I pray that each of you will follow the Lord with a passion and enjoy His blessing and direction in your lives.

I also extend my heart-felt gratitude to the leadership, the staff and the congregation of Gracepoint Gospel Fellowship, first of all, for allowing me to undertake this endeavor; secondly, for their love, support and prayers through these years of studies and especially through the days of facing a diagnosis of cancer and subsequent surgery. I have learned through this body of believers the richness that comes with diversity and my heart has been "enlarged" through them (2 Cor. 6:11). A huge thank you to Jeannie Kellum, and her mother Dolly, for hours spent in sifting through and tabulating surveys taken in the congregation early on in my Doctor of Ministry program that helped determine the direction of the project.

Finally, my appreciation to Dr. Michael Gregg, part of our delightful D. Min. cohort, who was pressed into service and worked with me consistently to edit and finish the project when there was not a lot of time left to get it done. Thanks Mike for helping to make it happen and thank you Dr. Pinkham for your encouragement along the way. Thanks to my daughter Kara for stepping up and entering in much of my data from the sorting task and to my son Daniel for converting pdfs to jpegs. A word of appreciation as well, to Maddie Cintron for perfecting the charts and compiling the final sorting data; also to my Business Administrator, right hand in the office, and friend of many years, Corinne Ambrosino for helping in the printing process, for proof-reading and picking up the slack of things I couldn't get to during this time. Lastly, my thanks to Dr. David Midwood, former President of Vision New England and long time friend, for stepping in as a reader of the doctoral project at the eleventh hour.

TABLE OF CONTENTS

CHAPTER ONE

A CHURCH DIVIDED

Eleven o'clock on Sunday morning is the most
segregated hour in America.
Dr. Billy Graham
Dr. Martin Luther King

Tragically, the last bastions of segregation in our society
are visible in funeral homes and churches. In too many
communities the church reflects the divisions existing
in society. Yet there are churches where the barriers of
racial enmity and mistrust have come tumbling down.
There are churches that transcend the difference of
color, national origin and even language.
Douglas Ruffle

My story begins with a transition that took place grad-
ually over thirty plus years of ministry in the same
church in Rockland County, New York. In 1977 I was called
to pastor New City Gospel Fellowship as a young man of
twenty-seven. The congregation was a "daughter church" of

a long established Pentecostal church in Bay Ridge, Brooklyn, an enclave of Norwegian immigrants. Thus the congregation, made up largely of displaced Brooklynites, was overwhelming families of Norwegian descent. How they ever determined that a Swede could lead and shepherd them is still a mystery to me. It must have been a "God-thing."

Nevertheless, as "lily white" as this congregation was in its inception, it was transformed over a thirty-year period to one of the most racially and ethnically diverse congregations found in the United States. By the year 2000, the makeup of the congregation was almost equally black, white and Hispanic with a sprinkling of Asian population. The uniqueness of this did not really register with me until, on several occasions when I described the makeup of the congregation, I would be asked, "How did that happen?" Pastors would often ask what we had done (assuming we had done something intentionally) to create such a phenomenon. Truthfully I was at a loss to explain what had happened. It was only as I began to research the topic of the multicultural church that I realized how unique an occurrence this in fact was.

The only hard data I could find came from a survey of George Barna, Christian pollster, par excellence, done in 1990. According to the Barna Research Group statistics, in modern America just three percent of the churches are integrated, that is, comprised of more than ten percent of a minority population – which certainly does not seem to be a very high standard. "Eighteen percent of churches have less than ten percent coming from races other than the majority" and seventy-nine percent of all congregations in America are mono-racial, leaving only twenty-one percent of churches as multicultural in the broadest sense of that term.[1] There has not been a more recent study by the Barna group to indicate whether or not these statistics are still valid or to what extent they have changed in the past two decades. George Yancey suggests a slightly different standard for "multiracial" churches. He defines a multiracial church as one where no one racial group makes up more than eighty per cent of the attendees. He concludes, using this standard, from a much more recent study (2003), that eight per cent of all American churches are multiracial.[2]

Over the past few decades, church growth specialists have suggested the "Homogeneous Unit Principle" (HUP) as one that will determine the growth and health of the local church. This principle states very simply that people are drawn to Christ and then to participation in a local church most frequently when that church offers a culture that is comfortable for them and does not require a great deal of change from their ethnic and cultural background. According to Donald McGavran, this principle is indisputable and evidenced around the world in the missionary enterprise of the church.

His words at the 1974 International Congress on World Evangelism were the following:

> The Christian Faith flows well within each piece of the mosaic, but tends to stop at linguistic and ethnic barriers. Most congregations are shut up to one language, one ethnic unit and frequently to one social or economic class.[3]

Elsewhere he states, "Men like to become Christians without crossing racial, linguistic or class barriers."[4]

Indeed, there is much to be said for this underlying assumption of the modern missionary and church growth movement. Donald McGavran, Peter Wagner, and others have extensively illustrated the principle in church growth materials. It is extremely difficult, if not impossible, for an individual to come to faith and then grow in his faith in a church where his primary (or his only language) is not spoken. It is also unlikely that an individual will commit to following after Christ when that act is seen as requiring a complete renunciation of the culture with which one is familiar and comfortable.

However, if this principle is used to suggest that churches in a multicultural society should continue to be segregated even when there is no linguistic barrier, so that people will be comfortable among their "own kind," then it would seem that an important New Testament principle and a dynamic of the gospel has been overlooked or compromised. The gospel of reconciliation has broken down the walls and barriers that naturally divide people in the world (Eph. 2:14-16). This gospel is meant to bring believers to an understanding of their unity and oneness in Christ, as well as of God's pleasure with their diversity and dissimilarity. This unity is not simply to be a theoretical matter but rather one that is visible in the church and noticeable to and perceived by the world.

Although the preaching of the gospel brought great diversity in the early church, overcoming some of the major divisions and hostilities of the society of that day, this characteristic of the church has often faded from view. Billy Graham's well-known remark, used by Dr. Martin Luther King Jr. as well, that eleven o'clock on Sunday morning is the most segregated hour in America, still rings true forty years later. Douglas Ruffle makes the point that in the late seventies a congregation with mixed races and nationalities was "a church in transition."[5] It was going from white to black or to Hispanic or Asian. Normally, when another race began to move into the neighborhood, or into the church, the reaction was "white flight," a departure of whites who often took their churches with them to the suburbs. Ruffle suggests that, tragically, the last bastions of segregation in our society are visible in funeral homes and churches. He notes the sad commentary that, "In too many communities the church reflects the divisions existing in society. Yet," he continues with hope, "there are churches where the barriers of racial enmity and mistrust have come tumbling down. There are churches that transcend the difference of color, national origin and even language."[6]

Meanwhile societies, both here and abroad, are changing rapidly. Demographic indicators point out that the United States is entering an era of greater diversity than ever before. Immigration from every continent is transforming the face of North America. Henry Wilson states, "Until 1960, about eighty percent of American immigration had come from Europe; since 1960, about eighty percent has come from places other than Europe. We are becoming what we had professed to be, the first universal nation."[7] The white non-Hispanic population of the United States dropped from seventy-six percent to sixty-nine percent in the decade leading to the year 2000. While the white population is projected to grow by three percent until 2050, the black race will grow by sixty-nine percent and the Asian and Hispanic populations by 195 and 199 percent respectively.[8] By 2050 fifty percent of the American population will be racial or ethnic minorities. The Asian population will have grown to 22 million by 2010 and the Caribbean and African black population will triple in the next five years. David Anderson, after supplying these statistics, challenges the church with these clever words: "If your vision for ministry doesn't include cultural diversity, your vision is not 20/20! It may be 1980's, 1990's or even 2005, but it is not 2020."[9]

Asante states that America was once a microcosm of European nationalities while today America is a microcosm of the world.[10] Social commentator Dinesh D'Souza observes:

> Each year some 800,000 legal immigrants and an unknown number of illegals enter the country. Unlike in the past, most immigrants do not come from Europe, but from Asia, Africa, and most of all from Latin America... If these trends continue, by the year 2050 whites will make up just 50 percent of the national population. Hispanics would be the largest minority, more than 20 percent and, counting illegals, possibly closer to 25 percent; blacks would be around 15 percent, and Asians near 10 percent.[11]

Immigration in the past primarily affected just six states. But according to the U.S. Census Bureau of Statistics, thirty-two of the fifty states experienced more than a 100% increase in their foreign-born population in the last fifteen years. In the first several years of this new century the nation has added some twenty million people, the vast majority being immigrants or their descendents.[12]

These changes seem to be leading to increased division, polarization, segmentation, and dissection of society and even to hostilities marked by increased aggression. Arthur Schlesinger suggests that the United States is in danger of losing its sense of uniqueness as competing ethnic groups each engage in retelling the American story from their own vantage point. He warns, "Ethnic and racial conflict will now replace the conflict of ideologies as the explosive issue of our times."[13] D'Souza declares, "Somehow the intended symphony has become cacophony."[14] The question is, will the church in America demonstrate more of the same or will the church be able to model convergence, harmony, reconciliation, and true fellowship to the world?

For a great number of white Americans, "the browning of America" is a fearful prospect as their power and sense of security is threatened. However, there are a significant number of Christians and congregations who see this trend as presenting great opportunity and potential for carrying out the missionary mandate of the church to "disciple the nations (*ethnos*)." This day in America can be viewed as a new Pentecost. Rather than having to travel overseas to reach people of other major religions and cultures, we are now encountering them throughout this country. Multitudes of non-Christians from parts of the world where there is little or no Christian witness are immigrating to the United States. Residents of a single Queens, New York zip code speak more than a hundred languages. National Geographic labeled Elmhurst 11373 the most ethnically mixed diverse zip code in the US.[15] Roger Sanjek notes the change in this community "from 1960 at 98 percent white, 1970 at 67 percent, 1980 at

34 percent, and 1990 to 18 percent white"[16] and refers to it as "The Future of Us All."

The mission field is no longer "remote." It surrounds us. Ray Bakke, who served as a Senior Associate with the Lausanne Committee for World Evangelization, agrees that the world at large is in motion and points out the implications for the church:

> In 1900, eight percent of the world's population lived in cities. By the year 2000 that number will be nearly 50 percent. . . . The majority of the world's non-Christians will not be geographically distant peoples, but culturally distant peoples who often reside together within the shadows of urban spires in the metro areas of every continent. Mission is no longer about crossing the oceans, jungles and deserts, but about crossing the streets of the world's cities. From now on, all ministries will be cross-cultural amid the urban pluralism caused by the greatest migration in human history from Southern hemispheres to the North, from East to West and above all, from rural to urban.[17]

Ethnic, social, cultural, and religious diversity has evolved in the major cities of North America and is even reaching our suburban and rural areas. A newsletter of Ramapo College in Bergen County, New Jersey, an affluent and historically white suburb of New York City, states, "The current increasing presence of immigrant people in Bergen County is a suburban phenomena."[18] Thus the opportunities for the church in

America to reach Muslims, Hindus, Buddhists, and those of other pagan religions are enormous. Toinette Eugene states,

> This country has seen a steady flow of immigrants and refugees from the very beginning. But the pace and variety have intensified . . . There are now parts of the country where no cultural group constitutes the majority of the local population. These changes affect not only the coasts and the big cities; even relatively homogeneous parts of the country now feel the tensions that the encounter between cultures can create . . . People in rural areas thus participate in the encounter (and sometimes clash) of peoples as much as those living in centers of direct immigration. The church is called to minister in these situations and is often unprepared to do so.[19]

Many Christians now have the chance to share their faith with peoples who in the past lived in distant countries often isolated and accessible only to the career missionary. They also have the prospect of inviting these peoples to come to church; thus the need for the church to be prepared to embrace and assimilate them into fellowship. McGavran, writing thirty years ago, stated:

> American Christian John Doe, who speaks English, earns $20,000 a year, lives in a middle-class home, and attends a typical congregation of about three hundred members, cannot win to Christ and bring into that congregation many Lebanese, Portuguese, Polish, French Canadian, Chinese or Indian immigrants to the United States. Even if they were to believe on Jesus Christ and be welcomed in that congregation, converts from these

and other ethnic units would not feel at home. If they came for one service, they would not likely return next Sunday. If they joined the church, they would be likely to drop out after a few months.[20]

The question today is: Do McGavran's premises continue to be valid today or have the societal changes since 1980 created a condition where the church indeed can reach out to a multiplicity of ethnic groups and assimilate them into its congregational life? Are there not many immigrants who welcome the opportunity to be "Americanized" and more importantly, are open to the Christian message, in this "foreign land"?

In a work written in 1979, Wagner strongly defended the homogeneous unit principle (HUP). After stating, "In a given American community, blacks may attend their kinds of churches, whites may attend their kinds of churches, and Hispanic-Americans may attend their kinds of churches," he then asks the question, "but does such separation please God?" Wagner comes down firmly on the side of the HUP by saying, "I hope to argue convincingly that ethical justification for homogeneous churches exists in social-psychological, theological, and biblical sources."[21] However, a decade later, Wagner made use of Bakke's research in his appeal to the church to target cities and he echoed the sentiment of Bakke in stating:

Traditionally, the geographically distant peoples have been the chief target of those we send to the mission field. But in today's cities, culturally distant peoples may be living in any neighborhood at all, and we are frequently blind to their existence as important targets for sharing the gospel. A first step is to see them as legitimate people groups who must be reached on their own terms or not be reached at all.[22]

He quotes Bakke as saying, "They will not be reached for Jesus Christ unless existing churches become multi-cultural by intention or unless user-friendly churches are started by and for them."[23] Wagner then continues with the challenge, "Anglo churches and other churches in urban areas should develop strategies for outreach which take the surrounding ethnic groups seriously."[24] Wagner then gives practical suggestions for encouraging this outreach.

Of course, many of the immigrants to this nation are already committed believers. Kathy Black says, "Many come with a rich Christian heritage, a celebrative spirit, and a deep commitment to both God and neighbor."[25] They are often more devoted to and more expressive of their beliefs and practices than the Christians of this country who have been so intimidated and marginalized by a secular society and distracted by materialism that they have repeatedly fallen into a indifferent and even monotonous experience in their Christian life. Believers from Africa, Korea, and from some of the nations where the church has been greatly persecuted have the potential of bringing a new vitality to the body of Christ here in America. Those who emigrate from other countries and cultures have a great contribution to make to the church of North America. Wilson suggests:

> Many immigrants come as enthusiastic Christians, and they will not be content to be members of an established congregation that has no room for their gifts and contributions. In other words, they will not linger around long if they do not experience a genuine integration through an appropriate transformation of the existing communities. That calls for a new approach, attitude, and openness on the part of the church.[26]

This observation brings to mind a host of questions. How will this movement of immigrants to our shores and our neighborhoods affect the make-up of local churches in the United States? Will local churches remain largely monoracial? Will the Christian immigrants remain in their own enclaves of spirituality separated from the rest of the body of Christ by language and cultural barriers? How will the changes of fifty plus years of civil rights legislation and political action alter, not only society, but also the church? How will the mobility of people in America and the integration of many neighborhoods affect church attendance?

The church in the United States in the twenty-first century has the opportunity to reverse hundreds of years of division, separation, and discrimination. Will the revolution begin or will the church be satisfied with the status quo? And, when and if churches begin to reflect the diversity of their neighborhoods and of society as a whole, will they enjoy the benefits and blessings of multiculturalism? "Will the churches in North America make use of these new vitalities brought by their Christian sisters and brothers who are now at their doorstep? Will they write off their evangelical fervor as charismatic, visionary and apocalyptic and keep them at a distance?"[27] Will the "fellowship of the saints" be simply a platitude found in a doctrinal statement or in a worship experience limited to the sanctuary? Or, will there be a connecting of lives from very different cultures and ethnic backgrounds in what the Bible speaks of as *koinonia* (fellowship), a true sharing of lives?

CHAPTER TWO

THE BIBLICAL – THEOLOGICAL BASIS FOR THE MULTICULTURAL CHURCH

(ೃ♋)

Thinking reconciliation precedes doing reconciliation.
Samuel Hines

Biblical and theological foundations are crucial to
support culturally conscious worship and the various
ministries of multicultural congregations . . . It is
even more important for multicultural congregations
because the society in which we live reinforces the
separation of races and cultures.
Kathy Black

Personal experience may play a key part in forming
convictions and commitments regarding issues of
culture and ethnicity. Far more significant, however,
must be a reading of Scripture.
Gary Parrett and S. Steve Kang

Many years ago, while in seminary, I was introduced to the Biblical concept of the Kingdom of God through the writings of George Ladd of Fuller Theological Seminary and especially through a classic work by John Bright entitled simply "The Kingdom of God." As a result, I began to see the Scriptures in a vastly different light and began to view the totality of Scripture through this lens of the Kingdom. More recently, as I began to look at the issue of the multicultural church, I have come to filter the Scriptures through the lens of "the nations." From Genesis to Revelation one can see the intention of God to reach the nations. His heart is inclined to draw the nations together in worship of the one true God and ultimately to display a unity of peoples in the midst of the tremendous diversity that he has created. The nations are everywhere prominent and conspicuous in God's revelation.

The hypothesis of this study is that key identifiable factors exist that lead minorities to attend and assimilate into a majority congregation or a diverse congregation. For any individual there are obstacles to involvement in a multicultural setting as opposed to remaining in more familiar and 'comfortable' surroundings. The church of Jesus Christ will benefit if these factors can be identified and understood. Once these factors are identified the question becomes how these dynamics can be encouraged and implemented in the local church. It is reasonable to suggest that the growth and multiplication of multicultural churches will ultimately be a major component in the evangelization of an urbanized multicultural society.

In this chapter I hope to give readers a taste of what it means to read the Scriptures in the light of, or through the lens of, this theme of "the nations." I have divided the examination of the Scriptures into traditional areas of theology including – ontology (dealing with the nature of God's being), anthropology (the study of the nature of man), Christology (the nature of Christ), soteriology (the nature of our salvation), ecclesiology (the nature of the Church), and eschatology (the study of the last days). Each of these areas of theology have been examined in order to recognize and respond to relevant and vital questions directly related to welcoming and assimilating those of various ethnicities into the local church setting. The goal is to set forth components of a theological worldview that can direct and sustain multicultural congregations.

My concern is to demonstrate the significance and practicality of the ageless Word of God and to develop a Biblical foundation for reconciliation between diverse people along with resulting implications for the life and ministry of the local church. The late preacher of reconciliation, Samuel Hines said, "Thinking reconciliation precedes doing reconciliation."[28] This statement points to a fundamental principle of the Christian faith. One must change his way of thinking before one can change his way of doing. "As a man thinks in his heart, so is he" (Prov. 23:7). Christianity is a matter of being rather than doing. A person is a Christian because of what he thinks and believes. However, correct behavior follows correct belief.

Kathy Black adds, "Biblical and theological foundations are crucial to support culturally-conscious worship and the various ministries of multicultural congregations . . . It is even more important for multicultural congregations because the society in which we live reinforces the separation of races and cultures."[29] Curtiss DeYoung comments, "A movement in Christianity toward more multiracial congregations in the United States will require a fundamental shift in belief systems and in organizational practices."[30] He quotes theologian Justo Gonzalez:

> The multicultural vision is sweet. But there is a bitter side to it. There is the side of having to declare that the vision of many peoples, many tribes, many nations, and many languages involves more than bringing a bit of color and folklore into our traditional worship services. It involves radical changes in the way we understand ourselves, and in the way we run our business.[31]

Ontological questions deal with the essence of God - His intrinsic character and attributes, as well as His essential way of being in relationship, that is, as a Triune Being. God is, according to Scripture and the orthodox creeds of the church, one and yet three. He is one God, eternally existent in three

40

persons, Father, Son, and Holy Spirit. These distinct persons relate to one another and may be seen as a 'community.' There is, in this Triune Being, an accord, a harmony, and a unity while there is yet diversity. "The trinity," David Ireland states, "is the perfect expression of unity with diversity."[32] The persons, though completely equal in power and identical in attributes, nevertheless display diversity in function and in relationship to one another. So it may be asked, "How has God's essential nature served as a model for mankind's relationships?" and "How has God's 'way of being' informed our understanding of unity and diversity?"

The anthropological issue focuses attention on the nature of man and causes one to reflect on the meaning of "the image of God" in man. It calls one to consider, "What is man that Thou art mindful of him?" (Psalm 8:4). Just as each person is to individually reflect the image of God in his/her attributes and character, so Mankind is to reflect God communally. What is the value of a human being? Are all of equal value? These significant questions can only be answered with reference to the origins of human life. Are all people the result of the direct creative act of a personal, loving God? Do all have an immortal soul? Are all descendents of the one man, Adam? Or are they in various stages of an evolutionary process where some are more advanced than others?

Christological concerns focus on the nature of Jesus and his work, his teaching and his ministry. We attempt to answer the question, "What did Jesus do?" when it comes to issues of race, ethnicity, and inclusion. Did the promised Messiah, who was son of Abraham and son of David, make room for people who were outside the scope of those historically known and recognized as the people of God? Did the One who came for the lost sheep of Israel show concern and compassion for those who were beyond the boundaries of that nation? Lastly, do we see the attitude and actions of the Savior replicated in His followers?

The subject of soteriology has to do with the nature of redemption and an understanding of reconciliation. What was lost in the fall of man, not only in his relationship with the Creator, but also in his relationship with his fellow human beings? How were those things restored in the work of Christ on the cross? Does the work of redemption restore man's relationship to man? Is it sufficient to be reconciled to God or is it even possible to be reconciled to God without being reconciled to our neighbor, or for that matter, to our "enemy"?

The ecclesiological matters revolve around the nature of fellowship and community. What was so radical about this early Christian community? What exactly are the responsibilities of members of the body of Christ to one another? How can Christ's followers duplicate the unity and harmony of

God's Being while not forfeiting their diversity? What, in fact, does it mean to be "a chosen people, a holy nation, a people belonging to God" taken from many peoples and nations? Can the concept of "separate but equal" work in the household of faith, or does that idea contradict the very essence of the gospel held onto by believers? Does the work of Christ include, not only the reconciliation of the individual to God, but also the reconciliation of man to man regardless of what has formerly divided and separated them? Does the quality of fellowship, love, and unity among Christians impact the effectiveness of the Body of Christ in evangelism?

Eschatological questions also have a bearing on the subject. One might ask whether the future hope of redemption lessens the hope of, or the need for, reconciliation in this church age? Is the "peaceful kingdom" portrayed by the Old Testament prophets a hope yet deferred? Or, is the paradise restored, as the prophets depicted it, something that can be realized and experienced within the church of Jesus Christ and the household of faith? The long debated issues of the millennial kingdom and the idea of "realized eschatology" are of consequence here. Eschatological issues relate to the nature of the Kingdom of God and whether or not it has already invaded the present through the advent of Jesus Christ and the outpouring of the Holy Spirit. How has the "already but not yet" aspect of the kingdom of God informed the nature of relationships among the congregants of the local church? Does the presence of the King and His Kingdom, though not fully consummated, offer new possibilities for and among His people that were not available prior to the arrival of the kingdom? How is the concept of forgiveness (a significant component for increasing fellowship and bringing about reconciliation and trust) to be understood in relationship to the arrival of the kingdom?[33]

Many of us in ministry and pastoral roles have neglected, in our preaching and teaching, matters related to race, issues of justice and discrimination, and the segregation of the body of Christ. The following discussion reflects this author's concerns and convictions regarding Biblical and theological issues related to the reconciliation of all men and women in Christ and the implications of that reconciliation in terms of their relationships and fellowship in the church of Christ. I hope to provide sermon material and to encourage pastors to address these issues directly from the pulpit. The following discussion will ask how these interracial relationships may be encouraged and friendships strengthened so that the members of the church of Jesus Christ may reflect the relationship that the Son has with the Father. Jesus' prayer was "so that they may be one as we are one" (John 17:11 NIV). He continued His request to the Father by saying, "My prayer is not for them alone. I pray also for those who will believe in me through their message, that all of them may be one" (v. 20, 21). His prayer was not only for the well-being of his disciples but also for the welfare of the church through the ages and ultimately for the benefit of the world: "May they be brought to complete unity to let the world know that you sent me and have loved them even as you have loved me" (v. 23). Evangelism will flourish when a lost and divided world sees an alternative to their experience in a redeemed and reconciled community in the church.

(1)The Nature of God's Being

Sound theology leads to good practice. In order to realize the goal of unity and reconciliation in the body of Christ, one must begin with a discussion of the very nature of God. An understanding of the nature of God and the implications of that knowledge is needed. Theology should never be relegated to abstract concepts about the transcendent One, but must be integrated into the very life and the relationships of the church. Julius Scott synthesizes:

> The Christian faith is not primarily a religion of doctrines, liturgies and laws . . . it is first and foremost a favorable, accepting relationship with God made possible through the person and work of Jesus Christ in accordance with the divine plan for redemption and reconciliation. It also involves relationships with others of like faith in the church community. This relationship with God, although it is not earned by human works

or behavior, has moral, ethical and social implications. The believer is to walk or behave worthily, in a manner appropriate to the nature and character of God with whom he or she is in relation. The Christian's goals, standards, attitudes and directives are the basic moral and spiritual principles that are rooted in the nature of God himself. "Good" is that which is in harmony with God's nature and which pleases him; wrong is that which is out of harmony with his nature and which displeases God.[34]

Triunity – The Basis of Diversity

It is imperative to know the nature of God. One cannot know Him apart from His revelation of Himself. Scriptural revelation makes it clear that He is one and yet He is three. The one true and living God is revealed as three persons. The doctrine of the Trinity demonstrates that God is, in Himself, a community. Mankind is intended to reflect God's likeness in this matter of community, experiencing harmony in diversity. Wayne Grudem says, "Because God in himself has both unity and diversity, it is not surprising that unity and diversity are also reflected in the human relationships he has established."[35] This community includes not only marriage and the family but also the church where there are many members with different gifts and abilities, as well as appearances, yet one body, "thereby demonstrating great diversity and great unity at the same time. When we see different people doing many different things in the life of a church we ought to thank God that this allows us to glorify him by reflecting something of the unity and diversity of the Trinity."[36] Larry Crabb adds the idea that the Trinity demonstrates "community at the highest level of reality" and the fact that "we were built for relationship."[37]

(If the following paragraph seems too abstract you may move forward to its conclusion in the next.) The orthodox formulation of the Trinity articulated at Constantinople was "one *ousia* (substance) in three *hypostases* (persons)." Erickson states, "the emphasis often seems to be more on the latter part of the formula, that is, on the separate existence of the three persons rather than on the one indivisible Godhead."[38] However, he declares, "The Godhead exists 'undivided in divided persons.' There is an 'identity of nature' in the three *hypostases*."[39] According to the Cappadocians of the fifth century (which included Basil the Great and Gregory of Nyssa), the individual persons of the Trinity are "related to the divine substance in the same fashion as individual humans are related to the universal human (or humanity). Each of the individual *hypostases* is the *ousia* of the Godhead distinguished by the characteristics or properties peculiar to him."[40]

In the same way individual humans share a common substance (*ousia*) or humanity but are distinguished from one another with unique characteristics. Just as the distinction of persons in the Trinity often overshadows their unity, so the differences between human beings often eclipse the oneness they enjoy. It is essential to emphasize the unity of God and also the unity of Mankind.[41] As the Trinity expresses unity in diversity so Mankind is made to reflect that unity in diversity. The attacks throughout church history on the doctrine of the Trinity have often led to an emphasis on the distinct persons within the Godhead. As a result the essential unity of the Godhead becomes almost secondary. In the same way, society's focus on diversity and individualism often causes men to lose sight of their essential unity. The multicultural church celebrates its diversity but must constantly focus on its unity and the likeness of its members.

God's Character - Divine Impartiality

Moral and spiritual principles emanating from God's being must be our directive for life lived in relationship with Him. The principles are as permanent and unchangeable as God. One must ask about the implications of God's nature for race relations and racial reconciliation.[42] We know the nature of God, not only through propositions about him, but through his dealings with mankind in history, through actions which display his character.

Scott focuses on one particular text, Acts 10:34, because it clearly links racial and cultural matters with a significant trait of God's nature.[43] Although Cornelius, as a Gentile, is considered from a Jewish perspective to be ceremonially unclean,

Peter is directed by a vision and by the voice of God to go to his home. He consents to go into the home although it is "against our law for a Jew to associate with a Gentile or to visit him" (v. 28 NIV). He finally gains understanding from the thrice-repeated instruction, "What God has cleansed you are not to call common" and he overcomes his lifelong perception of the Gentiles as unclean. When he enters the house of Cornelius, Peter says to this Roman centurion and to his companions, "In truth I perceive that *God shows no partiality, but in every nation whoever fears Him and works righteousness is accepted by Him*" (Acts 10:34, 35). Peter learns a lesson from a vision of unclean foods and applies the principle to people. This was a revelation of a "long-recognized aspect of God's nature that for Peter became the basis for attitudes and actions in a new situation."[44]

The impartiality of God is a theme occurring in both the Old and New Testaments and in early Christian literature. In the Law of Moses God is already declared to be one who is entirely impartial. "The Lord your God is God of gods and Lord of lords, the great God, mighty and awesome, *who shows no partiality*" (Deut. 10:17 NIV). This is reflected in the fact that He is just and fair to all regardless of social standing or ethnic background. Not only does He administer justice for the fatherless and the widow, but He also "loves the stranger" (v. 19). The word stranger (*ger*) in the text refers to the non-

Hebrew, a Gentile who is residing in the land of Israel. This is a remarkable affirmation, contradicting the sentiments of most of the Jewish people of later centuries. Kiel and Delitzsch comment on the passage in this manner,

> He does not regard the person . . . like a human judge. As such Jehovah does justice to the defenseless (orphan and widow), and exercises a loving care towards the stranger in his oppression. For this reason the Israelites were not to close their hearts egotistically against the stranger (cf. Ex. 22:21). This would show whether they possessed any love to God, and had circumcised their hearts (cf. 1 John iii. 10,17).[45]

All of the above is stated in the context of the covenant relationship between God and His people and the sign of that covenant. Israel is not only to circumcise the flesh as a sign of the covenant but also to circumcise the "foreskin" of their heart (Deut. 10:16); as Kiel and Delitzsch put it, "to lay aside all insensitivity of the heart to impressions from the love of God . . . Jehovah is mighty and terrible to all, without respect of persons, and at the same time a just Judge and loving Protector of the helpless and oppressed."[46] One obvious evidence of this act of consecration is that Israel will "love the stranger" as God does. God is just and fair and concerned for the weaker members of society. Thus He loves the foreigner. His people are to be and to do no less. "He will not tolerate haughtiness and stiffness of neck either toward Himself or toward other men."[47]

This same attribute of God is spoken of in 2 Chronicles 19:7 in the directive to the judges, "Let the fear of the Lord be upon you; take care and do it, for there is no iniquity (in this case, perversion of justice) with the Lord our God, *no partiality*, nor taking of bribes." Leaders are called to like character and to similar action. The "majority of uses of 'partial' or 'partiality' refer to improper discrimination against people in general or require fairness in judgment within God's covenant community."[48]

The divine ideal is encapsulated in the words of the scribes as they hypocritically but accurately complement Jesus with the words, "Teacher, we know that you speak and teach correctly, and *you are not partial to any*, but teach the way of God in truth" (Luke 20:21). The judgment day, according to Paul, will be a day demonstrating "no partiality with God" (Rom. 2:11; cf. Col. 3:25). Paul further states clearly that, "Whosoever believes in Him will not be disappointed" and reiterates, "Whosoever calls on the name of the Lord shall be saved" (Rom.10:9-13). The "whosoever" clearly eliminates any sense of discrimination on the part of God. "There is *no distinction* between Jew and Greek; the same Lord is Lord of all" (v. 12).

Impartiality Means Acceptance for All

Returning to Acts 10:34, one can see God's point is precisely that impartiality allows any and all to enter this new community of the King. Scott summarizes, "Ethnic background, race, culture, socioeconomic status, and the rest have no part to play. There are no external prerequisites for becoming a Christian, because God is impartial. There should be no requirements for membership in the church, the body of Christ, that God has not made for salvation."[49] Paul also insists that our unity in Christ means that distinctions of birth, class, and gender have no place in the church. "For you are all sons of God through faith in Christ Jesus. For as many of you as were baptized into Christ have put on Christ. There is neither Jew nor Greek, there is neither slave nor free, there is neither male nor female; for you are all one in Christ Jesus" (Gal. 3:26-28).

F. F. Bruce comments, "The cleavage between Jew and Gentile was for Judaism the most radical within the human race."[50] This verse in Galatians stands in particular contrast to the morning prayer of the Jewish rabbi where he thanks God that he is not a Gentile, or a slave, or a woman.[51] These distinctions that have considerable importance in Judaism are irrelevant in Christ. "The inferiority of slaves was marked enough in Jewish society," Bruce says, "but still more so in Mediterranean society generally and most of all in Roman

law."[52] Yet in the church the master-slave relationship is imma-
terial. It may very well be that Onesimus, the slave that Paul
writes on behalf of, became Onesimus the bishop of Ephesus
a half-century later.[53] Distinctions are not abolished in Christ,
but inequalities are. Our unity overcomes external divisions
and emanates from our relationship with Christ and with the
Father through Him. According to Scott, "Unity among God's
people is an extension and a reflection of God's nature."[54]

Since God is not a respecter of persons, there ought not
to be, on the church's part, discrimination against the slave
(Philemon 16), or inequity against the Hellenistic widows
(Acts 6), nor favoritism or preferential treatment for the
elders (1 Tim. 5:21), and no lesser treatment of the poor in
the church (James 2:1,9). These principles are echoed by the
Church Fathers (1 Clement 1:3; Epistle of Pseudo-Barnabus
4:12; Epistle of Polycarp 6:1). There will always be differences
of ethnicity, culture, social status, and economic situation.
These distinctions are part of what it means to be human, but
they do not result in preferential treatment on the part of God,
nor should they on our part.

For those who are in relationship with God, this unity
must, because of God's nature, take precedence over diversity. The simple fact is that for those who are "in Christ," such
distinctions, although recognized and acknowledged, should
not make a difference in relating to other human persons,

especially within the household of faith. To practice partiality is a denial of the nature of God and of the expectations of that God to whom the Christian lifestyle must be pleasing.[55]

Discrimination – The Denial of God's Image

The New Testament bears ample testimony to the fact that discrimination and division existed, even among believers. Whether differences were rooted in linguistic or cultural background (Acts 6), theological leaders or loyalties (1 Cor. 1), charismatic experiences (1 Cor. 12 – 14), social class (James 2:1-7) or for any other reason, the inspired writer, without trying to settle and sort out all the issues, says in effect, "Cut it out! Your unity, which is rooted in the impartiality of God and in the cross, must supersede any secondary, potentially divisive factors. You must learn to live accepting of diversity (of teachers and of giftings), knowing nothing among you except Jesus Christ, the crucified one" (1 Cor. 2:2, my expanded paraphrase on the basis of Paul's discussion in chapter one).[56] To do otherwise, as the epistle of James implies, is to operate on a basis unlike that which God used in choosing those who would be his own.[57]

Discrimination, on the basis of external factors, is wrong for those in relationship with God, as God Himself is not a respecter of persons. Within the framework of an appropriate Christian lifestyle, it is not necessary that all Christians adopt a common ethnic culture, strive for a uniform socio-economic level, have identical external religious experiences or learn from the same teachers. When fundamental theological, spiritual, or moral principles are not involved, diversity is acceptable and Christians should be sensitive to the preferences of their fellow believers.

Acceptance of human diversity may be difficult for many persons, including believers, but the New Testament writers base the necessity and the possibility of doing so on the impartial nature of God. The assumption is that those living in relationship with Him should not hold attitudes different from His. Furthermore, the awareness of His nature and the strength that comes from relationship with Him are sufficient to change both attitudes and behavior. The biblical writers assert that, when faced with the possibility of succumbing to prejudicial and discriminatory attitudes and behavior, the believer must make a conscious decision and effort to be and to do otherwise.[58]

In Acts 10:34 Peter says, "I now realize" or, "I grasp, I understand, I perceive or comprehend." He uses the present tense, depicting action in progress, which can thus be translated, "I am just now in the process of coming to realize for myself."[59] This change of heart is often a process rather than a moment of crisis. What blind spots are we harboring in our hearts, sometimes without even being conscious of them?

What Peter knew intellectually was now beginning to affect him existentially. Growth is a process. Peter began to recognize, to fully see, the impartiality of God and to understand the repercussions and ramifications of that in the mission of the church. He finally "got it."

(2) Man – The Image of God

In order to truly appreciate the concept of reconciliation we must understand God's original intention for man. What does it mean that man is created in the image of God (that he possesses the *Imago Dei*)? Erickson declares, "The image of God distinguishes us from all other creatures; it is what makes us human."[60] Grudem says, "Out of all the creatures God made, only one creature, man, is said to be made in the image of God . . . *thus man is like God and represents God*."[61] He goes on to state, "When the Creator of the universe wanted to create something 'in his image,' something more like himself than all the rest of creation, he made us. This realization will give us a profound sense of dignity and significance as we reflect on the excellence of all the rest of God's creation."[62]

Erickson goes on to elaborate on three different views of the image of God in man – the substantive, the relational, and the functional views. (The discussion of parts of this section may be too technical for some to enjoy. Try to stay with it.) The substantive view identifies the image with some definite quality or characteristic in man. It may be seen to be a physical, a spiritual, or psychological quality. Most often it is identified with man's reason. However, by identifying the image of God with reason, theologians have concentrated their attention on merely one facet of God's nature while isolating solely one aspect of human nature.[63]

The functional view, increasingly popular today, sees the image, not in something present in the make-up of man, but rather in something one does, such as the "exercise of dominion over creation."[64] Meanwhile, the relational view suggests that the image of God is the "experiencing of a relationship."[65] Neo-orthodox theologians Karl Barth and Emil Brunner both gave credence to this outlook. Erickson quotes them:

> The image of God is not to be understood in terms of any structural qualities within humanity; it is not something humans are or possess. Rather, the image is a matter of one's relationship to God; it is something one experiences. Thus it is dynamic rather than static. The relationship of humans to God, which constitutes the image of God, is paralleled by the relationship of one human to another.[66]

Humans alone, of all God's creatures, know God and are consciously related to Him. Man was made for communion with Him and sin disrupted that communion (Gen. 3). Both the Decalogue (Ex. 20) and the Great Commandments of

Christ (Matt. 22:36-40) focus on relationships with God and with people. To say, however, that this alone is the essence of the image of God cannot explain how the image of God is preserved in one who is indifferent to God or in outright rebellion against Him.

It would seem advantageous to understand the image of God through consideration of a combination of these views. Erickson summarizes in the following statements: The image of God is universal; it has not been lost as a result of sin, thus it is inseparably connected with humanity; it is not present in one man to a greater degree than another and it is not correlated with the development of relationships or with the exercise of dominion in any direct statement of Scripture.[67] Although the image of God in man has not been "lost" as a result of sin, one might see it as having been marred, distorted and tarnished.

Paul makes it clear that as a result of redemption the image of God is being restored in us. Christians are being conformed to the image of Christ where the image of God is seen perfectly in a human being (Rom. 8:29). What Christ is in his human nature is what man was intended to be. This includes the idea of relationship [note Christ's continuing intimacy with the Father while in the flesh (John 10:15,30; 17:21)], and the idea of authority [his control of the winds and the waves (Matt. 8:27) as well as his power over the demonic

(Mark 2:27)]. When Christ calmed the storm the question of the disciples was "What manner of man is this?" The answer appears to be, that having laid aside certain divine attributes and taking on human nature, he was still able to rule the elements and overcome the spirits of evil as a man dependent upon the Spirit. Thus His human nature is not the opposite of His divine nature but is truly a reflection of it. So will be our redeemed human nature. The image of God/Christ is being progressively restored.

Ericksen deduces that the image of God "should be thought of as primarily substantive or structural. The image is something in the very nature of humans. . . . It refers to something we are rather than something we have or do."[68] Therefore the relational and functional views ultimately focus on the "consequences or applications of the image rather than on the image itself."[69] Erickson then concludes that:

> The image refers to the elements in the makeup of human beings which enable the fulfillment of their destiny. The image is the powers of personality which make each human, like God, a being capable of interacting with other persons, of thinking and reflecting, and of willing freely. God's creation was for definite purposes. Humans were intended to know, love and obey God. They were to live in harmony with others . . . they were placed here upon earth to exercise dominion over the rest of creation. But these relationships and this function presuppose something else. We are most fully human when we are active in these relationships

and perform this function, for we are then fulfilling our *telos*, God's purpose for us. But these are the consequences or the applications of the image. The image itself is that set of qualities of God which, reflected in humans, make relationships and exercise of dominion possible.[70]

Although the substantive view of the image deals with the essence of God's image, the relational and functional views answer the question of what is the consequence or the manifestation of the image. Jesus, as perfect man, had perfect fellowship with the Father living in obedience to Him. He had an unconditional love, unselfish concern, and undying compassion for humans. Finally, we can agree, that we are truly and completely "human" only when manifesting the same characteristics we see in Christ.[71]

In the light of this discussion one can state unequivocally, the image of God is universal. Both sexes possess the image of God (Gen. 1:27; 5:1,2) and every ethnicity is included in God's family and thus reflects the image of their Father (Eph. 3:14f). The image is seen regardless of age or gender, marital or economic status, health or handicap, race or ethnicity. Therefore there is a dignity given to all human beings. All human life is valuable, even sacred. According to Erickson, "Because all are made in the image of God, nothing should be done which would encroach upon another's legitimate exercise of dominion. Freedom must not be taken from a human who has not forfeited this right by abusing it."[72]

Novak states, "God is infinite, and in order to mirror his infinity, all kinds and cultures of human beings are necessary."[73] Each culture illuminates some characteristic of God but no one culture can express all that God is. "Therefore, God is seen and understood better through a multiplicity of cultures than he could be through a mono-cultural humanity."[74] God reveals himself through special revelation (the Scriptures) and through general revelation (creation and nature). God has revealed aspects of Himself in the creation of man and in the diversity of mankind.

One Race – Many Nations

In Acts 17:24-29 one finds Paul's message from Mars Hill in Athens, a segment of which states, "from one man he has made every nation of men, that they should inhabit the earth; and he determined the times set for them and the exact places where they should live." His remark implies that there are not three or four races of mankind but one. Understanding creation aright, we speak of only one race - Adam's race, the human race. However, now as a result of sin and redemption, one may understand that there is the race of Adam and there is also the race of Christ. People are divided, not by skin color or DNA, but by belief. Humanity is not divided by ancestry but it is divided by faith.

God is the Creator of all Mankind. He created every one of us completely unique and strikingly different from all others. Greeley declares, "I would argue that the richness of human diversity is merely an aspect of the richness and superabundance of all creation, a manifestation of the overwhelming, overflowing goodness and power of the divine love."[75] Each one has his unique fingerprint, retinal print and DNA structure. Even when we are of the same ethnicity we are noticeably dissimilar in physical appearance and in personality. However, men are all incredibly similar as well. Even what appear to be major differences are not. Ken Hamm pronounces,

> These so-called 'racial characteristics' are only minor variations among the people groups. Scientists have found that if one were to take any two people from anywhere in the world, the basic genetic differences between these two people would typically be around 0.2 percent – even if they came from the same people group. But, these so-called 'racial' characteristics that many think are major differences (skin color, eye shape, etc.) account for only 6 percent of this 0.2 percent variation, which amounts to a mere 0.012 percent genetically.[76]

Thus "racial" differences are trivial, there being more variation within any group than there is between one group and another. In fact, variations in skin color can develop in just a few generations. Hamm quotes an ABC News science page that states, "What the facts show is that there are differences among us, but they stem from culture, not race."[77] John Orgunze refers to the Stanford Report when he states that genetic differences are better explained by geographical origin rather than by skin color and that there is no documented biological superiority of any race, nor is there "purity of the races anywhere."[78] Clara La Plante quotes Dill, "If we are going to take our spiritual life seriously, we have to subscribe to the monotheistic principle: A God who is one, and one humanity in the image and likeness of God. With every effort to overcome inferiority/superiority, which is an abomination whether it applies to race or gender, we have become closer to the kingdom of God."[79]

Cultural distinction is an act of God. "From one man he made every nation of men . . . he determined the times set for them and the exact places where they should live" (Acts 17:26). In other words, none of this was an accident. What God had placed in the DNA of Adam allowed for distinctions among his descendants. The sixth generation of Noah's descendants included two descendents by the name of Peleg and Eber (Gen. 10:25). The name Peleg means division and this is explained by a note in the Hebrew text, "for in his days the earth was divided."[80] The dividing of mankind was all in the plan and purpose of God.

Even that which resulted from the pride of man at the tower of Babel is to be considered an act of God and part of

His plan for Mankind. The tower of Babel was in fact man's attempt to stop the dispersion and the resulting diversity of nations that God had set in motion. The people of that day said, "Come, let us build ourselves a city . . . so that we may make a name for ourselves and *not be scattered* over the face of the whole earth" (Gen. 11:1,4). They were essentially rebelling against the cultural mandate of God to "multiply and fill the earth." The scattering of the peoples would increase the diversity of language, culture and in time, physical appearance. Commenting on this passage, Ireland expresses, "two things are evident: 1) that men were unified in their determination to prevent diversity and to maintain cultural and ethnic uniformity; and 2) that God was equally determined that diversity should develop. Such a battle of wills is, of course," according to Ireland, "no contest."[81]

This idea runs completely contrary to what is taught and believed in so many Christian circles. Many have simply looked at God's action in confusing the tongues and scattering the people abroad (Gen. 11:7,8) as an act of judgment. However, when we understand that the Lord was bringing about a diversity of languages and a scattering and division of peoples prior to this (Gen. 10:5), we recognize that God's judgment was upon the attempt to resist His planned diversity by building a unified city. God's original command was "Multiply and fill the earth." Diversity has always been in the purpose and plan of God and not a curse leveled on mankind. The dispersion of people was such an essential part of God's plan that man's resistance to it required an extraordinary intervention. God "came down," confused their language, and forced those building the tower and the city to be scattered all over the face of the earth. Diversity among nationalities, cultures, and ethnic groups was an indispensable ingredient in the plan of God regarding mankind.

St. Jerome, great theologian and translator of the Scriptures, concurs with this interpretation. He says, "Indeed, when the tower was being built up against God, those who were building it were disbanded for their own welfare. The conspiracy was evil. The dispersion was of true benefit even to those who were dispersed."[82] John Crysostom, bishop of Antioch in the fourth century agrees saying, "His purpose was that, just as similarity of language allowed their living together, so difference in language might cause dispersal among them."[83]

Every people group came from one source, Adam. A news article summarizes the admission of scientists that lends support to this Biblical truth. "Modern science, with the tools of DNA analysis, shows that all humans alive today share a common origin dating a few tens of thousands of years ago, an eye blink in evolutionary time. Superficial changes accumulated as people separated and spread around the world, some through chance and others through the need to adapt to different climates." The article continues, "There is no denying that people's physical appearance changes from one geographic region to the next. Skin color is the most dramatic such variable trait, but hair type, body form and facial features show patterns that coincide with a person's ancestry. What science does not find, however, are any sharp divisions between specific groups of people."[84] The Bible does not use the word 'race' in reference to different groups of people. There is truly but one race and that is the human race.[85]

Man was given the mandate to "multiply and fill the earth." All people groups are a part of the fulfillment of that mandate. The fulfillment of that mandate actually caused the variations in mankind. As they disbursed to inhabit remote parts of the earth, their unique characteristics were reproduced and multiplied in their descendents. Thus as time passed, those unique characteristics marked a people group as distinct from another. The news article written by Faye Flam quotes Kidd, a geneticist from Yale University who has compared DNA samples from people around the world, as saying, "Race is not biologically definable, we are far too similar." Despite this, he adds, "Race is a very real social construct" and thus the idea of race is not going to disappear.[86]

The famed botanist Carolus Linnaeus, known for his system of classifying plants and animals, declared that the human species was made of four sub-categories, which he labeled red, yellow, black, and white. This notion of separate human races has deeply ingrained itself in our culture with devastating consequences for many people throughout the world.[87] When we start with a premise contrary to the revelation of God, the philosophical, theological, and political dogmas that result can be terribly destructive. Consider the Nazism of Hitler and the Communism of Marx and Lenin. Darwin's theory of evolution allowed people to suggest that some men were more highly developed than others, allowing some to be categorized as animals - "soulless beasts." The result has been prejudice, discrimination, inequity, slavery, and even extermination of people groups who were considered sub-human.

A Chosen Race

Ireland concludes, "from God's perspective there are now two people-groups on the earth – two families that descended from two men."[88] "The first man Adam became a living being; the last Adam a life-giving spirit" (1 Cor. 15:45). We are either members of the lineage of the first Adam or of the lineage of the last Adam. Children of Christ are designated children of Abraham just as children of Adam may be referred to as children of the devil. Paul asserts, "Understand then, that those who believe are children of Abraham" (Gal. 3:7). " 'Abraham is our father,' the Pharisees answered. 'If you were Abraham's children,' Jesus said, 'then you would do the things Abraham did. . . . You belong to your father, the devil, and you want to carry out your father's desire' " (John 8:39,44). Ireland elaborates, "We are all in Adam by birth, and in Christ by faith. . . . God traces our ancestry in spiritual terms, not by blood relationships. . . . The Father categorizes people, not by natural pedigree, but by spiritual connection."[89]

The Jews were greatly prejudiced against the children of Hagar, the sons of Ishmael. They also discriminated against those known as Samaritans, who were less than "full-bred" Jews. In his letter to the Galatians, Paul took an old Pharisaic allegory and turned it on end (4:21-31). "Paul suggests that the Jews who rejected Christ were in fact the children of the bondwoman, Hagar. . . . Gentile believers were said to be the children of the free woman, Sarah," and thus the children of promise.[90] This perspective had the potential of infuriating the Jews.

In God's eyes all Christians are of the same race. "But you are *a chosen race*, a royal priesthood, a holy nation, a people for God's own possession" (1 Pet. 2:9). What Israel had been, the church now is. There is one race expressing inexhaustible variety. God has one family. He is the Father of all these children. In Christ, all physical, social, and economic characteristics by which believers could be categorized are eliminated.

"There is neither Jew nor Greek, there is neither slave nor free; there is neither male nor female; for you are all one in Christ Jesus" (Gal. 3:28). "There is no distinction between Greek and Jew, circumcised and uncircumcised, barbarian, Scythian, slave and freeman, but Christ is all and in all" (Col. 3:11). "For by one Spirit we were all baptized into one body, whether Jews or Greeks, whether slaves or free, and we were all made to drink of one Spirit. For the body is not one but many members" (1 Cor. 12:13f).

"God exists as a multiplicity with unity."[91] The triune God is One. "Hear O Israel, the Lord your God is one" (Deut. 6:4). The Hebrew for "one" in that text is *echad*, which signifies unity, oneness, but which can also demonstrate a plurality. It is the same word used in Genesis 2 to describe the union of the man and the woman. The two become one (*echad*) flesh. The covenant of marriage causes us to see two individuals as one. The covenant of salvation causes us to see two individual believers, of whatever ethnicity, united in Christ. Indeed all believers are united in Him. Jesus prayed, "that they all may be one, as You Father are in Me, and I in You" (John 17:21).

One cannot love God whom he has not seen and not love his brother who he has seen (1 John 4: 20). One cannot honor God and despise the temples in which he dwells.[92] "Don't you know that you are the temple of God and God's Spirit dwells in you? Do you not know that your body is a temple of the

69

Holy Spirit within you, whom you have from God?" (1 Cor. 3:16). The blessings of one's life and heritage are not given as symbols of superiority. They are bestowed so that one might bless the world. Jews, as people of God's special concern, thought they were superior to the nations. In fact they were called to serve and bless the nations. Jesus revealed that the Samaritan woman at the well had value; the Good Samaritan truly carried out the will of God; the Syro-Phoenician woman's cry was not ignored by the Master.

Both testaments repeatedly refer to God's plan for the nations. It first appears in the story of Abraham. His call came in order that the *nations* (plural), not one nation, would find blessing (Gen. 12:3). Jesus' Great Commission to his disciples likewise focuses on the *nations*. Disciples are to be made of all "*ethnos*" – all people groups. One is to lay aside preferences, prejudice, bigotry and any aversion to multiculturalism. Willingness to model inclusiveness in our lives and diversity in the local church is a dynamic testimony to the world.

The trend of the 1980's and 1990's was for people to define themselves "ethnocentrically." The world's population is dividing into smaller and smaller groups. We are becoming a world full of little gangs.[93] The world's concept of multiculturalism emphasizes differences and suggests tolerance and celebration of those differences. Within the church there is an added ingredient – that of "fellowship." This unique concept stresses the commonality that believers have in Christ despite the dissimilarities that are evident. It requires an unconditional love of one another. The believers in the early church held all things in common (Acts 2:44). This included material possessions as well as the apostle's doctrine and life lived "together" at the table and in prayer.

Ireland states, "being Christ-centered I could not be racially or culturally centered any more than I could be self-centered or money-centered... if I were ethnocentric then I could not live a life that is Christocentric."[94] Pero states, "As Christians we are no longer family centered nor ethnocentric. We are constantly confronted with the cross and the resurrection as we experience that water is thicker than blood. . . . No one is excluded here."[95] In a divided world, all Christians need to do to make an impact is simply to live and act like true Christians.[96] If we love people with the love of Christ and see all people as God sees them, the world will take notice. They will be open to our gospel of reconciliation.

(3) Jesus, the Reconciler
Minister of Reconciliation

One may ask, "Are multiracial congregations today a hoped-for outcome of Jesus' life work?"[97] So much of what Jesus did and taught, and even circumstances surrounding His coming, focuses on ethnic inclusion in a society and a day that was characterized by exclusion. Peart states, "The very life of Jesus is one that exudes reconciliation."[98] He quotes an apt and pithy saying of Athanasius, "Incarnation is reconciliation."[99] Other theologians have said, "Incarnation is divine enculturation as much as translation (Andrew F. Walls); it is divine immigration (Jung Young Lee)."[100] "Solivan posits that the incarnation requires, 'that divinity take on a foreign identity as flesh . . . our human existence.' "[101] Elizabeth Conde-Frazier suggests that we likewise, "are called to venture into the world of our neighbor, which may be different or even strange to us at times . . . The incarnation calls us to dislocate ourselves from that which is familiar and to relocate ourselves in fellowship with those who are different from us."[102]

The genealogy presented in Matthew's gospel included two Gentile women, Rahab the Canaanite and Ruth the Moabite, and possibly a third, Bathsheba, wife of Uriah the Hittite. Peart points out, "although His heritage was royal through the blood of the great Jewish King David, it was also universal through the blood of these women from two different ethnic groups."[103] DeYoung says, "Poor shepherds, whose line of work was despised by many in society, served as the primary witness to this historic event. The Gospel of Luke paints a picture of a Jesus who, even at his birth, experienced outsider status."[104] The arrival of the Magi from the east to prostrate themselves before the Christ child is a sign of the purpose of God to call all nations to the worship of the Savior. After His presentation at the Temple, the elderly and godly Simeon points to the role of this special child as an instrument of reconciliation to the nations: "for my eyes have seen your salvation that you have prepared in the presence of all peoples, a light for revelation to the *Gentiles*" (Luke 2:30-32). These words appear to be an allusion to Isaiah 52:10 where it is clear that God intends His salvation to be seen by "all the *nations*" and "all the ends of the earth." Luke's second volume, the Acts of the Apostles, records the fulfillment of this prophecy.

Jesus' earliest days brought him to the continent of Africa and are summarized in the statement "Out of Egypt I have called my son" (Matt. 2:15). Jesus the Jew was "raised in Galilee of the nations."[105] Matthew quotes the prophet Isaiah in introducing Him as the fulfillment of prophecy, "Land of Zebulun . . . in the latter time He will make glorious the way of the sea, across the Jordan, Galilee of the *Gentiles* – the people who sat in darkness have seen a great light" (Matt. 4:15-16). The diverse mix of people in Galilee reflected the demographics of much of the Roman Empire, and included Assyrians, Egyptians, Macedonians, Persians, Romans, Syrians, and indigenous Canaanites. Jesus certainly was influenced by this milieu.[106] Historian Barnett says:

His home was not the sacred temple-city, Jerusalem, the world center for the rabbinic academies but Nazareth in Galilee, a region surrounded by Greek states and permeated by Hellenism. It is appropriate that a message that was to be taken to the Gentile world should be centered on one who was nurtured and raised in Galilee of the Gentiles.[107]

A Message of Inclusion

Jesus' ministry and message is radically inclusive. His intention and willingness to touch individuals outside of his own ethnic group is clear in the gospels. Early in his ministry He responds to the request of a Roman centurion to heal his highly valued slave (Matt. 8:5-10; Luke 7:1-10). This foreigner is commended by Jesus and spoken of as a man of great faith. The Roman official states that he is not worthy to have Christ come under his roof but that, if Jesus will simply speak the word, his servant will be healed. It is clear from the text that it was Jesus' plan to go to the centurion's house even though, as we saw in the account of Peter in Acts 10:28, it was "unlawful for a Jew to associate with or to visit anyone of another nation." Jesus was able to distinguish between the laws of God and the traditions of men.

Likewise, a Canaanite woman is extolled for her great faith when she refuses to accept no for an answer as she anguishes over the demonic possession of her daughter (Matt. 15:21-28). The Canaanites were bitter enemies of the Jews since the Jews' entrance into the land centuries before. However, Jesus could not help but take action to bless this woman when she cried out for mercy. Her cry searched for an answer to the question, "Is there a God for those outside the family of a particular ethnic group and religion."[108] Jesus travels into what is a clearly Gentile territory (marked by the herd of pigs, animals that were unclean and avoided by the Jews). His mission there is eventually shown to be the deliverance of one demon-possessed stranger (Mark 5:1-20).[109] Jesus was also able, within his band of followers, to bring together a zealot, who was a fanatic for "Jewish nationalism," and a tax collector, who was seen as a traitor to the cause, thus bridging one of the great social chasms of the day.

It is apparent that one trip Jesus would not avoid was the journey through Samaria. Although He could have taken another route to evade contact with the despised Samaritan people, He rather chose to travel that way. Again, it appears that His purpose was to minister to the one person who, in the culture of the day, was to be avoided. He speaks to this woman although John makes it clear that normally "the Jews have no dealings with the Samaritans" (John 4:9). This woman, considered a social outcast because of her immorality and her race, is one of the few to whom Christ reveals His true identity. Jesus repeatedly acted contrary to "the religious and social taboos of His ethnic group to save a group of people with whom He was not supposed to associate."[110] Peart adds,

"These examples show us that Jesus was a minister of ethnic or racial reconciliation and was not satisfied in ministering only to those of his own ethnic group."[111]

DeYoung points out that Jesus had what might be referred to as a "table fellowship" with those that others refused to associate with:

> Table fellowship symbolized those you found to be worthy of inclusion in your social circle. Whom you ate with made a statement about who were your friends. The Pharisees were considered a 'table fellowship sect.' They used table fellowship to maintain the purity of their nation as well as to model what they believed should be the exclusive ethnocentric identity of Israel. Jesus disturbed and disrupted religious leaders of his time because he used table fellowship to model what he believed was the future of God's people (and who were included in that group).[112]

Whereas the Pharisees had long lists of those who were excluded from table fellowship, Jesus accepted tax collectors and sinners at His table. By accepting them "as friends and equals Jesus had taken away their shame, humiliation and guilt, . . . (he) gave them a sense of dignity, . . . made them feel clean and acceptable."[113] Borg writes, "Jesus did not simply accept the central role of table fellowship, but used it as a weapon. . . . It was a political act of national significance: to advocate and practice a different form of table fellowship was to protest the present structures of Israel."[114]

In a follow-up to the account of the Roman centurion, Christ's vision of the future is seen: "Many will come from the east and the west and will recline at table with Abraham" (Matt. 8:11). According to Christ, the nations from afar will feast with the patriarchs in the longed-for kingdom. Christ predicts a day when the Kingdom would be taken from Israel and given to a people producing its fruits (Matt. 21:43). This people would not be marked by natural descent but by the fruit of obedience and righteousness. Jesus, in the words of Wright, "was challenging Israel to be Israel; that is, to be the light of the world, the salt of the earth. . . . When YHWH finally acted for Israel, the Gentiles would be blessed as well."[115]

His teaching also reflects this inclusiveness. His preaching in the synagogue at Nazareth announces a ministry to the poor and oppressed (Luke 4:18). His illustrations include stories of the widow of Sidon and Naaman the leper, both from outside of Israel, who were touched by Israel's prophets. Such an approach got Him thrown out of the synagogue and nearly thrown off the cliff. The hero of one of His most loved and repeated stories is a Samaritan (Luke 10:30-37). This is akin, Peart interjects, "to an African-American having a white supremacist as his story's hero."[116] Most importantly, when Jesus gave the Great Commission to His disciples and delineated the purpose to which they were to devote their lives, the *nations* were at the center of that charge. His followers were to make disciples of all *ethnos* by baptizing and teaching them (Matt. 28:19). It is obvious that the impartiality of the God of Israel is incarnated and revealed in the life, ministry, and teaching of his unique and beloved Son.

(4) The Nature of Salvation

There are various images used in the Scriptures to describe the work of salvation. The words atonement and propitiation are sacrificial terminology. They focus on the vicarious or substitutionary element in salvation. Redemption is a figure of speech from the marketplace. It focuses on a price paid and an object that is bought back after being lost. These are familiar concepts in both testaments. Another image used is that of reconciliation which may be seen as a figure of warfare.[117] There are parties that are opposed to one another. They are enemies, adversaries, hostile to one another, each seeking to do harm to the other. The word reconciliation has to do with the removal of that hostility and a change of attitude that allows the coming together of the two in harmony and in one accord. Enemies become friends. The cause of animosity is eliminated and the wall of division is removed. According to Verlyn Verbrugge, "Reconciliation denotes the end of a relation of enmity and the substitution of one of peace and goodwill."[118]

Reconciliation – An Essential Element

The term 'reconcile' is not frequently used in the New Testament yet it "remains a basic theological term that defines vital aspects of the salvation that God offers us in Christ."[119] It is "among the basic concepts of Pauline theology," serving to "give greater theological precision to Christ and His work than the soteriological concepts found in the Synoptic Gospels and Acts (e.g., forgiveness)."[120] The root word *allasso* simply means change or alteration.[121] Various compounds of this, including *katalasso* and *apokatalasso* (verbs), and *katallage* (noun) word are translated 'reconcile/reconciliation'. The word refers to a change in tone that Paul desires to make with regard to the Galatians (Gal. 4:20). It describes the transforming of the believer's body on the Last Day (1 Cor. 15:51) and the change wrought in the heavens by Christ when the world is destroyed (Heb. 1:12).[122] The compound word *apokatalasso* stresses the completeness of the restoration effected (Col. 1:20, 21).[123]

Therefore the words translated 'reconcile' or 'reconciliation' focus on a change – in personal relationships between human beings, or between human beings and God.[124] Hines puts it in these terms, "The word most frequently translated "reconciliation' in the New Testament literally means to change completely, thoroughly or radically."[125] The word describes our new relationship with God (2 Cor. 5:18; Rom.

5:10) as well as a transformed relationship of one person to another (e.g., a wife to a husband, 1 Cor. 7:11).[126] Relationships that were strained and broken are no longer, having experienced reconciliation (a change) - a complete or dramatic revolution.

There are four important New Testament passages which speak of the work of Christ under the figure of reconciliation, namely, Romans 5:10f.; 2 Corinthians 5:18ff.; Ephesians 2:11ff.; Colossians 1:19ff. Persons being reconciled were formerly hostile to one another. We were at odds with our Creator. Richards notes, "Objectively and psychologically we are placed in a position of hostility, at enmity with One whose only desire is to express His love."[127] The Bible does not soften the message when it states that we are sinners and that sinners are 'enemies' of God facing His wrath (Rom. 5:10; Col. 1:21; James 4:4). We should not minimize the seriousness of these passages. An enemy is not someone who comes up just a little short of being a friend. He is in the other camp. He is altogether in opposition.

But now a change has taken place. Whatever it was that caused the hostility has been eradicated. The Bible pictures God in strong opposition to everything that is evil. He is vigorously opposed to the sin in one's life while at the same time He cares for each person. He must do something to eradicate sin so that sinners are not left facing His wrath. He does this in Christ, where Christ actually becomes sin for us (2 Cor. 5:20), that is, a sin offering, that incurs the wrath of God in our place. The fire of God's judgment comes upon Him on the cross. God found in the death of His Son "a way for His love for the sinner and His wrath against sin to be accommodated."[128] Christ died to put away man's sins so that they no longer are counted against him. Thus He has justified us and He has also dealt with the enmity, that which stood between man and God. By making man the "righteousness of God," He opened the way for men to come back to God. This action is embodied in the term 'reconciliation.' "Biblical reconciliation comes through the atoning work of Jesus Christ on the cross."[129]

No New Testament passage speaks of God being reconciled to man. The direction always is that men are reconciled to God. "For if, when we were God's enemies, we were reconciled to Him through the death of His Son, how much more, having been reconciled (*katallasso*), shall we be saved through his life" (Rom. 5:10 NIV). This in the nature of the case is very important. Richards states, "It is human beings who need reconciliation; their sinful attitude toward God needs to be changed."[130] It is man's sin that has caused the enmity and the distance. It is man in sin that needs to be absolved. Man is called upon to "be reconciled to God" (2 Cor. 5:20).

Scholars at times suggest that Christ's reconciling activities are concerned only with man, that they influence his attitudes, and constrain him to turn to God. But it is difficult to harmonize this interpretation with the general New Testament position. That which sets up the barrier is the of God's holiness for uprightness in man. Man may not appear to be concerned about his sin or to openly demonstrate hostility to God. The obstacle arises because God demands holiness in man. Man exhibits hostility to God when he is conscious of and/or resistant to that demand.

Therefore, when the process of reconciliation has been effected, it is impossible to say it is completely man-ward, and not God-ward in any sense. There must be a change from God's side if 'the wrath of God' is no longer exercised and directed towards man. Verbrugge notes, "The subject of reconciliation is God." He continues, "Note the contrast to pagan thought, which knew the deity only as the object of the reconciling work of humans. At the same time it is consistent with the Old Testament message of God as the 'compassionate and gracious' one, who reveals 'love and faithfulness' as belonging to His very being."[131] We must think of reconciliation as being effected by God and as having influence in both a God-ward and a man-ward direction.

Reconciliation was initially effected without man's input and prior to anything happening within man. Paul can speak of Christ "through whom we have now received our reconciliation" (Rom. 5:11). A reconciliation that can be 'received' must be proffered (and thus in some sense accomplished) before men receive it. Again Verbrugge, "Human action, including repentance and confession of sins, is not a work we do to bring about and initiate reconciliation, to which God reacts. Rather, it is God's work, to which we must react."[132] Reconciliation is effected through Christ's work in His death and resurrection. Paul usually describes the effect with the words justification and righteousness. "The fact that *katallasso* and *katallage* can be used in parallel with these terms (cf. Rom. 5:9 with 5:10; 2 Cor. 5:19 with Rom. 4:3-22) indicates the central place these words have in the preaching and theology of Paul."[133] Reconciliation is God's gift. "All this is from God, who reconciled us to himself" (2 Cor. 5:18 NIV). But it does not end there. We are now called to a ministry of reconciliation. We are Christ's ambassadors. God is "making His appeal through us" (v. 20). This appeal is in the gospel message. The message of reconciliation is the word of the cross. To proclaim it is the responsibility of the whole church.

Throughout the central portion of the letter of 2 Corinthians (5:11-7:4), Paul deals with this "ministry of reconciliation." C. K. Barrett says that in this part of the letter "Paul's thought moves paradoxically between the treasure of the Gospel and the mean earthenware vessel in which it is contained - the message and the messenger" and he labels the paragraph (5:11-21) as "one of the most pregnant, difficult, and important in the whole of the Pauline literature."[134] Paul appeals to the Corinthians to be reconciled to God (5:20) but also to open their hearts to him, their apostle (6:13). He clears the way for these appeals by first responding to criticisms of the style of His ministry (5:11-15) and then by stating the theological basis upon which reconciliation rests (5:16-21). He then makes his appeals (6:1-13; 7:2-4), interspersing them with a call for holy living (6:14-7:1). So reconciliation in this passage focuses on our relationship with God but the discussion is prompted by a prejudice, even a hostility, against the apostle due to his style of ministry and the need for reconciliation between Paul and the Corinthian believers.

Paul is forced to defend himself. He lets the church in Corinth know that he could not do anything other than serve Christ. He is striving to serve with the utmost integrity, for it is the very love of Christ that compels him, that "controls our actions" (5:14). He is convinced that Christ died in his stead, and now he wants to live for Him. We see two aspects of Paul's motivation for ministry, each of which ought to be reflected in the believer's motivation to serve the Lord. On the one hand, Paul is aware of his accountability to God and so has a healthy fear (v. 11). On the other, he knows of the great love of Christ and so cannot do otherwise than live for the one who died and rose for him (vv. 14-15).

Before continuing his appeal to the Corinthians, Paul makes a succinct but extremely profound statement about the work of Christ: "God made Him who had no sin to be sin for us" (v. 21). Various interpretations of this have been suggested: 1) that Christ was made a sinner; 2) that He was made a sin offering; 3) that He was made to bear the consequences of our sins. The first suggestion is to be rightly rejected out of hand running contrary to the many Scriptures that point to his sinlessness. The second can be supported by appeal to Paul's use of sacrificial terminology elsewhere (cf. Rom. 3:25; 1 Cor. 5:7) and to the fact that in the Greek version (the Septuagint) of Leviticus 4:24 and 5:12 the word is used to mean *sin offering*. The third interpretation is supported by appeal to Galatians 3:13, where Paul speaks of the death of Christ in terms of His bearing the consequences of our sins: "Christ redeemed us from the curse of the law by becoming a curse for us, for it is written: 'Cursed is everyone who is hung on a tree.' "

The last interpretation is also supported by the fact that the statement, "God made him who had no sin to become sin for us," is balanced by the complementary statement, "so that in Him we might become the righteousness of God." If 'becoming the righteousness of God' means that God has pronounced judgment in our favor and put us in right relationship with God, then to 'become sin,' as the opposite of that, would mean that God had pronounced judgment against Christ when He took upon Himself the burden of man's sin (cf. Is. 53:4-6, 12). As a result, His relationship with God was momentarily, but horribly, severed (*cf.* Mt. 27:46) for us. It is then no wonder that the love of Christ was such a strong motivating force in Paul's life. Once grasped, the significance of Paul's love of Christ will also be a strong motivating force in the lives of present day believers.

The Horizontal Dimension

Paul's ministry, like the ministry of Christ, reflects a concern for reconciliation among men. One result of the momentous change occasioned by Christ's death and resurrection is that Paul has a totally new outlook. "From now on," he says, "we regard no one according to the flesh" (KJV) or "from a worldly point of view" (2 Cor. 5:16 NIV). Barrett says that "according to the flesh" has the meaning "that one's estimates are based upon purely human, and especially self-regarding, considerations."[135] Hughes suggests that:

> from the time of his conversion and enlightenment by the Holy Spirit, his (Paul's) knowledge, by which he means his appraisal and acknowledgement, of persons is no longer, as it once was, after the flesh – in other words, in accordance with the estimate formed of people by the unregenerate man and the world in

general. The world's standard of value is respect of persons in their outward appearance. . . . But with God there is no such respect of persons (Rom. 2:11; Eph. 6:9; Col. 3:25).[136]

Attributes and achievements that formerly were extremely significant to Paul, he now regards as unimportant (cf. Phil. 3:4-8).

First of all he regards Christ in a new way. "Though we have known Christ according to the flesh, yet now we know Him in this way no longer" (2 Cor. 5:16b). Paul is not saying that he has no interest in the Jesus of history.[137] Rather, he is saying that in his pre–conversion days he judged Christ using worldly criteria and came to the wrong conclusion. He does so no longer. The significance of Christ's action is seen in the fact that "if anyone is in Christ, he is a new creation, so that it may be said, the old has gone, the new has come!" (v. 17). Hughes says, "A man in Christ is a creature entirely renewed, for whom the old judgments after the flesh have become a thing of the past (v. 17). He now knows Christ as He truly is."[138] To be in Christ is to be participating already in the new creation, to be brought into the *eschaton*. Now we have revelation from God - "a new kind of knowledge."[139] It is true that for the time being the old still persists and the new has not yet fully come (cf. Rom. 8:18-25; Gal. 5:16-26).

In other words, Paul says, "Now I see Christ differently." Hughes remarks, "prior to his conversion his knowledge of

Christ had been after the flesh, formed in accordance with external and mistaken standards; but his conversion had meant the transformation of his knowledge of Christ."[140] The New Living Translation reads, "How differently I think about Him now!" Paul seems to imply, "Once I mistakenly thought of Christ as though he were merely human, a pretender and a fraud, a false Messiah." Just as he now has a different view of Christ so he has a modified view of all men. As Christians we have ceased evaluating Christ and others from a worldly perspective. Fraser states, "The basic meaning is that Paul, with others, had new fuller understanding of the 'whole Christ' by the Spirit and by faith; and he sees others in a new way according to their standing with Him, in the new eschatological situation, in the 'new creation.' "[141] Hines says,

> Reconciliation is God's idea. Therefore, our thoughts must conform to the mind of God. Until we can think God's thoughts, we will struggle uselessly in our attempts to act as God would act in a given situation. The reconciler recognizes and believes that reconciliation is God's one-item agenda. God is the author of reconciliation. People only carry out the reconciling process that God initiated. Reconciliation begins between God and human beings, through the atonement of Jesus Christ, and then is channeled through us to each other by the empowerment of the Holy Spirit. Many reconciling projects are only of brief duration because the doers cannot think in God's terms.[142]

Thus there is not only a vertical, but also a horizontal element, involved in reconciliation. It is not solely about properly aligning one's theology or Christology but also about one's relationships. In Christ one's perceptions and judgments are corrected and my prejudice is removed. Prejudice relates to drawing conclusions about another before examining the facts, before really knowing the person. A person may once have mistakenly visualized Jesus as a mere man. Jews were perceived to be less than human by the Nazis; Blacks have been seen as inferior to Whites. But in Christ one can say, "How differently I think about Him now!" and also "How differently I think of them now!" Hughes encapsulates, "Typically worldly distinctions, such as those of race, social status, wealth and title, should no longer govern the Christian's estimate of his fellow-men (cf. Gal. 3:28)."[143]

The word respect means to value, to esteem, to reverence, to have a high opinion of another. Etymologically however, it is "re" meaning again and "*spect*" suggesting what is seen (a spectacle is an event seen or witnessed; an instrument for seeing it; spectacular connotes something impressive to observe; a spectator is one who watches). Therefore to have respect means to "look again," "to see in a different light." The person, that once was perceived as a monster, a leech, an animal, is now recognized as one made in the image of God.

Paul writes, "How differently I think about Christ now" and about other people as well. His perspective has changed. He once judged on the basis of limited facts, understanding, and perceptions. Now he sees differently. Do we? Or do some of the old ways of seeing persist? Hughes concludes in his discussion of this passage, "Yet it is sadly possible for those who profess the faith of Christ to estimate others according to the flesh."[144] "Man looks at the outward appearance but God looks on the heart" (1 Sam. 16:7). One is not to treat others on the basis of their outward appearance or their obvious wealth (James 2:1-4). This passage instructs us to take others at face value (the word James uses is literally "take face").[145] One is to view others as does God.

Ephesians 2:16ff completes the picture of reconciliation in the New Testament. Not only have individual persons been reconciled to God and called to proclaim this truth but reconciliation has affected ethnic groups in their relationships with one another. It affects both Jews and Gentiles. Gentiles, who were once "separated from Christ, excluded from citizenship in Israel and foreigners to the covenants of the promise, without hope and without God in the world" (v. 12 NIV), are now "brought near through the blood of Christ" (v. 13). In Christ Jews also have a means of salvation they did not previously realize. "At the same time the act of reconciling Jew and Gentile to God reconciles them to each other and creates a new humanity, 'one new man out of the two, thus making peace, and in this body to reconcile (*apokatallasso*) both of them to God through the cross.' "[146]

Paul speaks of "the barrier, the dividing wall of hostility" (v. 14). At the temple in Jerusalem there literally was such a wall. Around the temple one wall or partition separated the innermost Court of Israel from the Court of the Women and another such wall separated the Court of the Women from the Court of the Gentiles. Only Jewish men could enter the Court of Israel while Jews, both male and female could go into the Court of the Women. Gentiles were not allowed past the outer partition. On that dividing wall hung a sign with a warning. This inscription, a notice from Herod's Temple discovered by archaeologists in 1871, read: "*No man of another nation is to enter within the fence and enclosure round the temple. Whoever is caught will have himself to blame that his death ensues.*"[147] These words are indicative of the separation and the animosity between Jew and Gentile. It demonstrates the unwillingness of the Jew to accept and embrace Gentiles as fellow worshippers. It is this attitude of hostility and exclusion that the message of reconciliation destroys.

People are often found to be in opposition to those of other races and ethnicities. It is not simply an indifference or neglect but hostility, antagonism, and anger resulting in aggression and violence. Larry Richards comments, "Mankind is now a divided race, shattered by hostilities that are precipitated by such distinctions as color, sex, social status, and cultural background." He also states, "Paul points out that Jew and Gentile, separated by multiplied hostilities and diverse outlooks are now joined 'in this one body.' "[148] Strangers and foreigners become fellow citizens and members of God's household. The way to overcome enmity is to remove the cause of the division. This is what Christ accomplished. One may apologize for a hasty word, one may pay back the money that is due, one may make what reparation or restitution is appropriate. But in every case the path to reconciliation involves an effective grappling with the root cause of the enmity. What is the root cause of enmity between the races? It is pride and prejudice. The message of reconciliation deals with the enmity between God and man and also with the enmity among men.

One may ask the question "Is the call to reconciliation optional or is it a mandate?" Paul implores, even commands the Corinthians, "Be reconciled to God!" Reconciliation to God is a calling. It is a command. It is the core of the gospel. Reconciliation with man is no less a calling and command of God (2 Cor. 5:16-21; Mark 11:17; Acts 21:27-22:22; Eph. 2:11, 12). Hines summarizes, "Reconciliation is the way of the cross – love pressing its way even in the face of death. We must take the path our Savior took . . . reconciliation transcends all humanly motivated efforts to get people together."[149]

Reconciliation – The Church's Mission

Peart states, "For as reconciliation, both spiritual and racial, was an integral aspect of Jesus' purpose on earth, we also find it to be an integral aspect of the church's purpose."[150] In the Acts of the Apostles, often referred to as "The Acts of the Holy Spirit," but probably best named, "The Acts of Jesus by the Apostles through the Holy Spirit," the early church encounters resistance to the attaining of this goal. Throughout the struggle, the Spirit is at work as the agent of reconciliation. Peart adds, "Clearly whenever the unity of the church was threatened by questions of a cultural, personal, or doctrinal nature, it was the Holy Spirit who was identified as working to bring the different groups together."[151] Peart highlights the centrality of racial reconciliation to the church's purpose by examining the church's mission, message, mark and measure of success.[152]

The mission is the Great Commission. It is to disciple the *nations* (Matt. 28:19), to preach repentance and forgiveness in his name to *all nations* (Luke 24:47). It is to begin at Jerusalem but reach the *"uttermost parts* of the earth" (Acts 1:8). Although the *glossolalia* of the disciples on the day of Pentecost is directed only to Jews, it is a preview of what is to come since these Jews are pilgrims who are characterized as "devout men from *every nation* under heaven" (Acts 2:5). DeYoung notes:

On the day of Pentecost the Jerusalem congregation grew from 120 Galilean Jews to over 3,000 multicultural, multilingual Jews (2:41). . . . The church was multicultural and multilingual from the first moment of its existence. . . . Congregations of the church of God from Jerusalem to Antioch to Rome embraced people from a wide range of ethnic backgrounds and cultural perspectives, becoming houses of prayer for all the nations. They were implementing Jesus' instruction to make disciples from all the nations. The diverse and inclusive nature of early congregations did not occur by accident. This outcome was a result of embracing the vision and strategy of Jesus.[153]

Their hearing of the gospel and their response to it is a foretaste of the coming advance of the gospel around the world. These individuals were able to hear the apostles speaking the "wonders of God in their own tongues" (Acts 2:11). Peter's message later emphasizes that this "promise is for them and their children and for all who are *far off*" (Acts 2:39).

"Differences bring challenges, conflict and tension. The Jerusalem congregation learned this early."[154] The first challenge faced within the church was the discrimination displayed when certain widows were overlooked in the distribution of food. Prejudice reared its ugly head in the church as the Aramaic-speaking Jews in the church neglected the Greek-speaking widows. It was the matter of cultural and linguistic differences that led to preferences and partiality. Men of the Spirit and of wisdom were called on to eradicate these injustices and to avoid ethnically divided congregations.

Those who were chosen bore Greek names. The wisdom of the church was evident as they chose men from among the marginalized group to solve the problem. They could most effectively deal with the injustice experienced by the Greek-speaking widows. DeYoung adds, "The Jerusalem congregation faced head-on the challenges posed by diversity with action that was prayerful, immediate, empowering, and that further implemented Jesus' vision."[155]

Afterward we see the progression of the gospel through Philip to Samaria, then through Peter to the Gentile Cornelius and finally through Paul to the Gentile world to whom he was specifically called. Peter can only become a part of this mission when he realizes that the church is to be a reflection of God's character in that it cannot show partiality.[156] The proof of God's acceptance of the Gentile believers is the Holy Spirit's falling on them. Peart summarizes:

> Clearly the nature and mission of the church is different than what the Jews had come to accept as God's modus operandi. The church is to have a universal mission that brings all people into a reconciling relationship with God and with one another (Acts 11:1-18; Eph. 2:1-22). As Peter learned, and later taught other Jewish church leaders in Jerusalem, ethnic diversity is an integral attribute of the church's mission.[157]

(5) The Church's Message

Like the message of Christ, the message of the church is an impartial invitation. Peter sums up, "God is not willing that any should perish but that *all men* should come to repentance" (2 Pet. 3:9). Paul voices that God our Savior "desires *all people* to be saved and to come to a knowledge of the truth" (1 Tim. 2:4), that "there is no distinction between Jew and Greek; the same Lord is Lord *of all*" (Rom. 10: 12). The apostle cannot seem to stress this invitation to the nations enough as he concludes his great epistle to the Romans. He repeatedly quotes the Old Testament in making the point that Christ not only confirms the promises given to the patriarchs, but becomes a servant in order that the *Gentiles* might glorify God for his mercy: "As it is written, I will praise you among the *Gentiles* . . . Rejoice, O *Gentiles*, with his people . . . Praise the Lord, *all you Gentiles*, and let *all the peoples* extol him . . . the root of Jesse will come, even he who arises to rule the *Gentiles*; in him will the *Gentiles* hope" (Rom. 15:8-12).

It is to achieve this goal that Paul states he has been commissioned by God (Acts 22:21). He does not hesitate to proclaim this fact even when the expression of that purpose might cost him his life at the hands of a Jewish mob. In the narrative recorded in Acts 21 and 22 the Jews at the temple seized Paul and a riot ensued. The Roman soldiers had to restore order after which Paul was given permission to speak. He got the attention of the Jews when he spoke to them in Hebrew. He held their attention for some time while giving his testimony until he stated (according to Acts 22:21 NIV), "The Lord said to me, 'Go; I will send you far away to the *Gentiles*.' " The text then adds, "up to this word they listened to him." When Paul came to that word "*Gentile*" the crowd went wild. They wanted to do away with Paul for suggesting that God was interested in and concerned for the *nations*. However, their threats did not sway him from his "*Gentile mission*." He was absolutely convinced that this aspect of the gospel could not be eliminated from the message. "The gospel message," Peart concludes, "is far beyond the social, cultural, political, and even religious norms the world holds. We must proclaim the standards that God has set – that all people are called to a relationship with God and with one another that is uniquely different from what they have ever experienced."[158]

The Mark of the Church

Research suggests that congregations begun in Galilee included Gentiles as well as Samaritans. The tendency toward establishing congregations that reconciled Jews and Gentiles became the standard of the early church.[159] DeYoung quotes Rhoads' summary of the first century church:

> The early Christian movement meant nothing less than breaking down the dividing wall between Jew and

97

Gentile. And this universal vision was much more than the combining of two groups, for neither was monolithic. On the one side, Judaism was itself multiform in that era of history. . . . On the other side, there was a multiplicity of Gentile nations. . . . Across the ancient Mediterranean world, there was an incredible array of local ethnic communities, subcultures, and language groups within the aegis of the Roman Empire. . . . These Jewish groups and Gentile nations comprised the multiplicity of cultures that Christianity sought to address and embrace.[160]

The missionary movement of the church, and particularly the work of the apostle Paul, resulted in multiethnic churches in cities like Antioch, Philippi, Thessalonica, Corinth, and Ephesus. Antioch, a metropolis of its day, was marked by ethnic diversity, poverty, crime, homelessness, slavery, and ethnic strife. Stark describes it as "a city filled with hatred and fear rooted in intense ethnic antagonisms and exacerbated by a constant stream of strangers."[161] Barnabus and Saul were linked with Simeon, called Niger (meaning black), Lucius of Cyrene (one who came from northern Africa), and Manean, a member of the court of Herod. This was obviously a diverse leadership team for the fledgling assembly begun there. This assembly lived out an inclusive table fellowship. In the midst of Antioch's ethnic pressure "Christianity offered a new basis for social solidarity."[162] It was here that they were first called Christians. DeYoung quotes Elizondo:

This name declared that they made up 'a social but not an ethnic group'.... the Christians could not be classified according to the classification categories of either the pagans or the Jews. They were both and yet they were neither the one nor the other alone. They were the same and yet they lived differently. They were bound together by a new intimacy and mutual concern that went beyond normal, acceptable behavior within the empire.[163]

The one mark or characteristic of the church that Jesus prayed would be manifest is unity (John 17:20-23). When there was a threat to the unity of the church in Jerusalem, the Holy Spirit worked through Spirit-filled men to achieve peace. One of those men was Philip who was then used of God to communicate the gospel first to the despised Samaritans and then to a foreigner - an Ethiopian government official. The conversion of this individual no doubt marked the opening of an entire people to the reception of the gospel.

There was potential for division in Antioch when Peter withdrew from table fellowship with Gentile believers, so Paul publicly opposed him. Once again we hear from DeYoung:

Paul chose not to take what seemed the pragmatic course of action, that of 'founding a separate and exclusively Gentile church.' The apostle Paul 'never wavered in his conviction that God was making a new creation by drawing into one church both Jews and Gentiles.' He believed that it was not enough just to maintain a spiritual unity in the universal church. Unity needed to be seen and experienced in the local congregation as well. The break in sharing meals together would end 'the social unity of the church.' The apostle Paul could not stand by and allow the Christian church to lose its power to reconcile and therefore make void the truth of the gospel.[164]

The apostles apparently were not satisfied with homogeneous churches. The mixing of the cultures presented challenges but none too great for the work of the Spirit to overcome. The heterogeneous church was no impediment to the spread of the gospel.

The Realization of the Mission

Lastly, the measure of the success of the mission is ultimately seen in the accomplishment of the mission. For this one needs to turn to the final chapter of God's revelation – John's apocalypse. There, diversity is the character of the eternal Kingdom (Rev. 7:9). The greatest witness to the effectiveness of Christ's sacrifice is when people from *every nation* worship together. The triumphant multitude is one that "no one could number." These words, Stephen Mott explains:

> are an exact quotation of Genesis 13:16 and 15:5. God's promise to Abraham that his offspring would be too numerous to be counted is fulfilled in this multicultural body redeemed by Christ. The mission of the Abrahamic covenant, which becomes the mission of the church, to be a blessing to all the families of the earth, is linked to the multiplication of his offspring (Genesis 22:17-18). The Revelation of John has per-

ceived that the promise is not merely the number of descendents but also one of diversity. Abraham would be 'the ancestor of a multitude of nations' (Gen. 17:4).[165]

What should be the construct of the church on earth? It should resemble heaven. "Thy will be done on earth as it is in heaven." Christians are to rejoice in diversity. It exalts Jesus as *Lord of the nations*. He is not a tribal deity. Mott notes, "Human efforts to keep cultural units separate or to disparage particular ones are shown to be out of keeping with God's final working in history. Since these distinctions are retained in this new creation, they are revealed as part of God's creative intent, but not as grounds of sinful evaluation or discrimination."[166]

When Jesus prayed for his followers he "focused on one mark, or characteristic, that they would need to manifest (John 17:20-23)."[167] Though he could have chosen any number of traits to describe his covenant community, he decided to focus on unity "because it best reflected a characteristic of God that the world was sure to note, a unity that went beyond the earthly differences that so commonly separated people."[168]

Robin Gill adds:

> to deny the spiritual unity and equality of men is utterly to deny the Bible; while to deny that this unity is and must be manifest in the visible Church, to admit apartness in the visible Church though not in the Spirit, would be equally to deny the Incarnation, that the Son of God lived among men, and his Church a fellow-

ship of men on earth, an eating and drinking society, a physical cum spiritual communion.[169]

(6) The Prophetic Vision

(Note: This last section will inevitably be a controversial one since eschatology is the doctrine that divides Evangelicals more than any other. I would ask the reader, even if you disagree with the eschatological view expressed here, to read on with an open mind. I believe that there is something that even the one who holds a contrary view might glean from the discussion. And who knows but that by the end of the discussion you might agree with me on points where you did not before.)

The Jews, after experiencing centuries of oppression and defeat at the hand of their enemies, became disillusioned with "this age." They anticipated "the age to come," an age of peace and righteousness and a day of vindication, spoken of by the prophets. They saw the direct and ultimate intervention of God as the only hope for their people. This perspective is given voice in the Jewish apocalyptic writings in the centuries preceding and immediately following the coming of Christ. The hope of a better world was seen beyond the cataclysm of the end.

Much of the evangelical church has likewise seen the only real hope of a better world as coming after the return of Christ. Many of the Old Testament promises of a Kingdom of peace and righteousness are seen as being fulfilled only in heaven or in a millennial Kingdom established on earth with Christ seated on an earthly throne reigning from Jerusalem. For the most part, Evangelicals today have subscribed to either a historic pre-millennial view of eschatology or a more recent dispensational version of pre-millennialism. However, the amillennial view has not been without its advocates, particularly in Reformed circles. It has support among many theological giants of the church including Augustine, Luther, Calvin, the Princeton greats and others. The term a-millennial (literally meaning no millennium) is really a misnomer with the term "realized millennial view" being a better one.[170]

The term "realized eschatology" is one that conveys the idea that the Kingdom of God is present in the person of Jesus Christ and in the work of His Spirit. The church is realizing the coming of His reign, the Kingdom, in this present age. According to this view the apocalyptic intervention of God began in the first coming of Christ and in the outpouring of the Holy Spirit. The age of the church is seen as the fulfillment of many of the prophecies of the Old Testament. As the popularity of the dispensational position seems to be waning among many Evangelicals, there appears to be an increasing emphasis on the Kingdom and its present reality in the Church and in the ministry of the Holy Spirit.

The Dispensational idea that the Kingdom was offered to and rejected by the Jewish people and thus that it has been "postponed," has led to the extreme idea that much of the teaching of Jesus (such as the Sermon on the Mount) is for a future millennial age and is thus irrelevant to the church today. This has resulted in great loss to the Church. In the same way, Old Testament prophecy has often been relegated to a place of irrelevance, being seen as descriptive of that far off, future age rather than the present church age.

Two passages of Scripture that have frequently been used to support the idea of a future, earthly reign of Christ on earth are Isaiah chapters 2 and 11. The latter of these depicts an idyllic paradise where the wolf and lamb dwell together, the leopard and goat lie down next to each other, and the calf, even a calf fattened for slaughter, reclines with the lion. The cow and the bear graze alongside one another. Furthermore a little child is able to lead these ferocious beasts while an infant plays over the hole of the cobra with no threat of danger. The picture is summed up in the words "They shall not hurt or destroy in all my holy mountain" (Isa. 11:9 NIV). The pre-millennial view asserts that it is obvious this scene has not been fulfilled, nor will it be in the world, as we know it. Therefore a day is coming on this earth when nature will be transformed. Certainly a "literal" view of the text demands such a conclusion.

However, if one approaches the prophetic word as an apocalyptic text (certainly a genre of writing that is evident elsewhere in Scripture), one filled with symbolism, then one might see the prophet pointing to the age in which we now live – the church age. Then the transformation observed here is not about the beasts of the field. It is rather a makeover and transformation of those who are "predators" and "victims" by nature. The Law of Moses allowed oxen to eat when treading out the grain (Deut. 25:4). Paul uses this verse to make a case for the preacher or apostle receiving a salary. He says, "Does not the Law say the same thing?" (1 Cor. 9:8). He asks "Is it for oxen that God is concerned?" Paul is suggesting in this passage that the original Word from God in the Law spoke of more than God's concern for beasts. Implied in the text, he says, is God's greater concern for the preacher. He makes a leap from the dumb beast to preachers of the gospel when he asks and then answers the question. His illustration moves from the beast to the man without any qualms. Is it then far-fetched to say that the prophet (or the Spirit of God speaking through the prophet) had in mind men and women who are predators and victims, just as the Law of Moses ultimately contained a principle applying to men (preachers) when speaking of oxen?

In the Isaiah passage it may be said, groups of people or individuals (symbolized by the lion) lose their aggressiveness, their ferocity and belligerence and their desire to do away with others. The predatory nature which harms and destroys is tempered and altered. This is the transformation of the new creation that Paul speaks of. On the other hand, the lamb's instinct is to run. He must learn to be strong and stand as an equal. Those who were once victims are no longer the oppressed and subjugated; those exploited and taken advantage of are now living in security without fear. Eric Law suggests that, "If we stretch the analogy of the 'wolf and lamb' scenario further, one might say that the cultures of the world are as numerous as the kinds of animals inhabiting this world. Each culture has its own characteristics, values, and customs. Some are perceived as strong and some as weak. Some are more aggressive and some are considered passive and timid."[171] Thus this passage can be seen as a vision of culturally diverse peoples living together in harmony and peace. Law concludes, "Very 'unnatural' behaviors are required from all who are involved. How can a wolf, a leopard, a lion not attack a lamb, a calf or a child for food?" He continues,

> Perhaps we have to go against the instinct of our cultures for us to stop replaying the fierce-devouring-the-small scenario of intercultural encounter. Perhaps, when all of us have learned how to do that, we may be able to regain our innocence like a child playing over the hole of the asp and putting her hand on the adder's den and not being afraid anymore.[172]

The holy mountain in the Old Testament is the temple mount. However, in the New Testament it is an image used by the author of Hebrews to speak of the church of Jesus Christ (12:22). It is not a geographical location but a place where men and women no longer seek to hurt and injure or to dominate for self-gain; rather their goal is to "fill the earth with the knowledge of the Lord as the waters cover the sea" (Isa. 11:9). The root of Jesse, the Messiah, stands as a banner for the peoples in that day. "The nations will rally to him and his place of rest will be glorious" (v. 10). Law adds, "As Christians, we are often called to go against our instinct. Jesus Christ invites us to take up the cross and follow him . . . to take up the cross – an instrument of the cruelest capital punishment."[173] This is to go against our instinct, "to uncover our own cultural waters, and to live in the uncharted intercultural waters of the Peaceable Realm."[174]

The *nations* stream toward the mountain (Isa. 2:2). They come to this "mountain," the church of Jesus Christ, in order to learn of His ways and walk in His paths. The law goes out from Zion and the word of the Lord from Jerusalem. The writer of Hebrews also uses Zion and Jerusalem as figures of the church (Heb. 12:25). One may see the ministry of the church in teaching and preaching previewed here. Reading on, the Messiah is in view, as are the nations: "He shall judge between the *nations* and settle disputes for many *peoples*." The verse is not looking at nations as we think of them, with political boundaries, but rather people groups who would naturally be at odds with one another and hostile in their interactions, having little in common culturally, but finding a point of unity in Him.

The result is that they lay down their swords, even beating them into plowshares. Instruments of war and destruction become instruments of harvest and of blessing. The propensity of peoples to attack one another (with the sword) is transformed into a desire to build one another up, to reap a harvest (using the plowshare). Spears are shaped into pruning hooks. The weapons of anger, rage, malice, slander and filthy language, so characteristic of us before Messiah intervenes, are now transformed into compassion, kindness, humility, gentleness, and patience (Col. 3:9-12). Today the Messianic Jew and the born-again Arab are brothers, partners and friends. Likewise are the Korean and Japanese, the Northern and Southern Irishmen, the Black and the White, those who have been touched by the transforming Spirit of God.

The central eschatological hope of the church is the *parousia*, the second coming of Christ. Andrew Park suggests, "The notion of *parousia* has shaped Christians' attitudes toward history."[175] He criticizes the church for simply waiting for the physical return, often setting dates. Rather than fulfilling history Christians have spent time negating history. Awaiting the glorious return, and seeing little hope for this age, many followers of Christ have not even attempted to transform society. The Church has misled many in predictions of the second coming and has often sapped her own strength.[176] He concludes, "When one has a healthy vision of the *parousia,* one can see the right direction for one's mission in the world."[177]

The gospel writers focus on preparation for the last day. One will not know the day or the hour of his coming. That is unimportant. One should not be caught up in "signs." One needs, at whatever time he lives in human history, however close or far from the consummation, to prepare for His return through righteous and faithful living. Jesus instructed us to "occupy until he comes." "Occupying" is not a passive word but rather gives the sense of an occupying army that is vigilant, alert for danger, constantly discerning the threats of the enemy. The parables of the wicked servants, the wise and foolish bridesmaids, and the rich fool imply that the fools are those who do nothing to prepare. Those who use their talents are sensible. One who hides them is not prepared for the master's return. The one with her lamp trimmed and filled with oil is wise. The key to Christ's teaching on the end of time is the theme of preparedness and faithful service while one is waiting the coming of the Lord (Matt. 24:42ff; Matt. 25).

Christians have often been preoccupied with the physical coming. However, Christ comes to His people continuously.[178] There is a personal, visible and physical return at the end of human history and there is the invisible, spiritual coming of Christ throughout history. Jesus says, "I am coming soon" and He says "I am with you always." *Parousia* can mean both "coming" and "presence." Many miss the fact that He is present in "the least of these" (Matt. 25:40, 45). He appears in and through the disinherited and the suffering. Park speaks of a *"parousia* from below," rather than from above. This is the *parousia* of Christ in the form of the downtrodden. Parks affirms:

> The success of spreading the gospel hinges on how we treat our neighbors, particularly our ethnic neighbors. If we regard them as strangers, we are still on the road to Emmaus. If we see them as inferior beings, we come to despise Christ. If we see them as the coming of Christ, Christ resides in us. Christ arrives in the oppressed peoples.[179]

There must be a transformation of our hearts causing us to treat the least of these "as Christ in history."[180] Park wraps up the revolutionary thought with these words, *"Parousia* is not the end of the world but the beginning of a new world. We need more people who will usher in the *parousia*, not just wait for it; those who will advance the arrival of the *parousia*."[181]

The Distant Future - A Worshiping Host

In Revelation 7:9f John presents a grand vision of multicultural worship, of how things appear in the eternal kingdom:

"After this I looked, and behold, a great multitude that no one could number, from every nation, from all tribes and peoples and languages, standing before the throne and before the Lamb, clothed in white robes, with palm branches in their hands, crying 'Salvation belongs to our God, who sits on the throne, and to the Lamb!' " In this splendid host, Stephen Mott says:

> The stress is on the ethnic and cultural inclusiveness of this multitude. Nation (*ethnos*) refers not to a political unit but to a cultural nation, bound by similar language, culture, and ethnic patterns. A tribe (*phyle*) derives its unity from genealogical and family bonds. In the Greek Old Testament (the Septuagint), a people (*laos*) frequently meant people which had a distinctive basis of unity. Language (*glossa*) is often the most striking characteristic distinguishing a cultural unit. John's primary point is the international inclusiveness of the redeemed people. It is striking, however, that he does not describe the inclusiveness simply in the standard New Testament terms of Jew and Gentile. Instead the inclusiveness is said to be drawn from every multicultural unit . . . none is to be excluded or elevated. Any attempt to do so is in conflict with this ultimate inclusion in the vindicated band. Their distinct identities are retained, however; yet they have been united, first in martyrdom and then more gloriously in the worship of God and in the comfort God gives.[182]

Is this not also how things should look in the church in the present day? Paul indicates that the church is a people "upon whom the end (the fulfillment) of the ages has come" (1 Cor.

10:11). Can His body not realize the future envisioned in the Apocalypse in the here and now? Experiencing and demonstrating that will impact the world and testify to the power of the gospel to transform human relations. Are the images seen in John's apocalypse only for the distant future or are these representations showing the church something of God's will and intent for His people now?

An apocalypse is a revealing of something that was previously hidden. It is not just that which is future. Paul speaks of the "mystery made known," that which was previously hidden, now revealed by the Spirit to the apostles and prophets (Eph. 3:3-5). That "mystery" was that the Gentiles should be fellow heirs with the Jews, "members of the same body . . . according to the eternal purpose which He accomplished in Christ Jesus our Lord" (v. 3:3-11). The ideal future presented in the Apocalypse is invading the present in the church. The new creation is being realized in those who are even now that "new creation in Christ."

The vision of multicultural worship seen in Revelation, the "apocalypse of worship," can be perceived in the mind of Jesus. Blount and Tisdale state that particularly in the gospel of Mark:

> Jesus is a preacher of multicultural worship. He envisioned a future that was radically different from the one espoused by the Temple leadership of His present

Jerusalem. The temple presided over a world where non-Jewish ethnicities were condemned by the theological motifs of holiness and purity, and demonized by the myopic fever of messianic nationalism."[183]

The Jews had seized on the themes, taken from the Law of Moses, of contamination, defilement, and separateness and had made these issues their main concerns. They used these theological ideas to rationalize their lack of involvement with and concern for the foreigner. According to the Law of Moses, those who were defiled could not approach the tabernacle or enter into the presence of God. Those individuals were to be avoided so that they would not defile any one else. Jesus' ministry revealed that exposure to and the touching of the defiled would not contaminate a person. Instead, one who was holy could have a purifying effect on the unclean and even bring about their wholeness. In Jesus' person and teaching one sees the presence of God approaching the tainted to restore them to health, wholeness and holiness.

In Jesus' day there were two courtyards surrounding the temple where Jewish men and Jewish women respectively were allowed. Gentiles were limited to the outermost court. This would certainly have been the place where the buyers and sellers of sacrifices, as well as the moneychangers, would do business. It was here that Jesus "cleansed the temple." Jesus then offered a 'counter kingdom' proposal. He foresaw a time when people of *every nation* would call God's temple their house of prayer. He was able to see what John viewed in his vision – every tribe and tongue gathered around the throne in worship. It is evident that Jesus visualized the apocalypse of worship, the revelation of this end-time reality which is God's reality. So Mark's purpose in recording and relaying this incident is to rally the disciples of Jesus toward this end. Mark wanted them to bring into the present what Jesus had foreseen and what John will ultimately foresee of the end.[184]

Mark's gospel begins with Jesus' preaching, "The time has come; the Kingdom of God is near (at hand, imminent). Repent and believe" (Mark 1:14-15). With His first words, Jesus declares that the present is being invaded by the future. The future, God's rule, has arrived in our midst. He identifies this future as the Kingdom of God. He later declares that it is a mystery (4:10-12) but that the disciples will see and know truths about the Kingdom that others will miss. Jesus' own person represents the reality of that future in the midst of the present. That is to say, His campaign of teaching, healing the sick, raising the dead, and casting out demons represents the reality of heaven on earth. It is God's invasion of divine power and transformation coming into the now.[185]

The Gospel of Mark is not what people expect of an apocalypse. The gospel reveals the future, the Kingdom of God, through its presentation of Jesus, but the unveiling is not one of "extraordinary mythological creatures, end-time calculations, number puzzles, or deterministic countdowns" as we see in The Apocalypse.[186] It has no otherworldly journey where a seer escapes the conflicts of the present age by warping forward into a future.[187] Mark's apocalypse is historical. Its most pressing interest is in the problems that occur within human history. This historical apocalypse promotes the determined assurance that God will bring about a real-time, historical, and transforming intervention. In the Jewish apocalyptic writings this world is totally unredeemable and will therefore be destroyed. In this historical apocalypse, Blount notes, "Though the present and the future remain two distinct ages, the future brings its power to bear in such a way that it not only salvages the present it also transforms it."[188]

In the Old Testament we find the Israelite codes of purity. Rhoades states, "The notion of holiness is rooted in two concepts: wholeness and set-apartness."[189] There are boundaries between those who are people of God and those who are not, as well as between groups within the people of God – those who are whole and those who are broken.[190] Leprous skin, spilled semen, blood, or even spit may contaminate. People are separated, due to these issues, into categories of clean and unclean.[191]

In such a context worship is a monochromatic affair – only those who are whole are welcome. There are categories of clean and unclean – some are in and some are, regrettably, but necessarily, out. Neyrey says, "The prime activity of a group with a strong purity system will be the making and maintenance of these lines and boundaries."[192] This system of holiness served Israel well throughout its history, preserving a minority culture from absorption into dominant cultures. At the time of Jesus, the culture and religion of the Jews were threatened with assimilation into the dominant Greek culture and with decimation by the imperialism of the Roman Empire. The Jewish understanding of purity protected the people from these threats of cultural domination. By keeping themselves separate from the Gentiles, the Jews maintained their beliefs and practices.

National and religious survival depended on separateness. There was infrastructure in place to protect from conquest by armaments or by ideas. In Jesus' time, the symbol of that system was the Jerusalem temple. The key to survival seemed to be the plan to "maintain the boundaries." This explains the severity of the warnings posted at the entrances to the temple sanctuary and court. Gentiles went beyond the barrier under threat of death. A threat to the temple was considered a threat to the social and religious fabric of the nation.

Participation in God's future hinged on allegiance to God's desire for holiness and purity in the present (Dan. 1:8; 3:12; 7:18, 22, 27; 12:10). To worship a holy God in the future one must be prepared by being set apart from uncleanness now. The Jews understood this to mean that every other culture and people, were by definition, unholy. Worship was, by their definition, always mono-cultural.[193] The Jews built up boundaries. Particularly in Mark's gospel, Jesus appears to tear them down. He transgresses the boundaries and is a transformer of thought.[194]

Jesus almost gives the impression that He is on a quest for contamination. The synagogue in Capernaum appears as a "monochromatic" clean room. However, it is in reality in need of cleansing. It is there Jesus encounters the demon-possessed man (1:23). Later, when confronted with the leper, He lays hands on forbidden, diseased skin (1:41). Instead of becoming infected Himself, He heals the skin and makes the leper whole. Sinners meet in Christ the power of forgiveness (2:1-12). Others count His claim as blasphemy but He has appropriated to Himself a power of cleansing reserved only for God. "Jesus is not moving into impure realms where He ought not to be, He is claiming God's power to transform them."[195]

Blount states, "in contrast to the view that people are to attain holiness by separation from the threatening force of impurity, Mark presents the view that people are to overcome uncleanness by spreading wholeness."[196] Jesus has table fellowship with the tax collectors, another group considered by the Jews to be impure (2:13-17). Healing is for the sick, not for those who are already whole (v. 17). Human wholeness is more important than cultic observance and ritual rightness.[197] Some want to "stop this intrusion of the future into the present."[198]

Jesus not only challenges Israel's internal boundaries, He also goes beyond the external limits that separate the holy people of God from the unholy group of communities surrounding them. In Mark 5 He sails across the lake to the Gadarenes, confronting one possessed by demons in the tombs, the place of the dead. He sends the unclean spirits into the unclean pigs so that the man can be cleansed and made whole. The transformed man proclaims the message of Christ's deliverance throughout the Decapolis, a region of Gentiles (v. 20). In Mark 7 Jesus challenges the Mosaic food laws. He eats at an inclusive table. The table is a representation of community. By proclaiming all foods clean, He suggests that the Gentiles, as well as the food they consumed, had a place at the table of God's kingdom people (cf. Acts 10:15). They too could become a part of God's "holy" community (cf. Matt. 8:11). In Mark 7:24-30 He embarks on a Gentile mission into Tyre and Sidon. He ministers to a Syro-Phoenician woman. It is in the Decapolis, around the Gentile cities, that the loaves are multiplied apparently for thousands of *Gentiles* (7:31-8:9). Bread is available to Gentiles – as is healing.[199]

The Near Future - A House of Prayer for All the Nations

If we continue this examination of Mark's gospel we come the most crucial text of all in this matter. The bastion of Israelite holiness and purity is the Jerusalem temple (Mark 11:12-25). Approaching the temple one day, Jesus is hungry. He looks to a fig tree for fruit. There is none. The fig tree was a symbol of Israel among the prophets. Jesus expected fruit from the tree as God the Father did from the nation. Each is disappointed. Jesus curses the tree. When they approach the temple precincts the next day Peter recognizes the tree and declares that it is withered. The account of the temple cleansing is, not accidentally, surrounded by this story. The temple is also fruitless. In reality it is the nation that is truly unproductive. The temple has failed to become what Isaiah said God intended it to be, "a house of prayer for all nations." It has 'leafy traditions' - codes of holiness, but the hunger expressed by the prophet for a place of prayer where all were welcome remains unsatisfied.

Jesus echoed the concern of the Law of Moses and the prophets for the stranger, the foreigner, and the nations. Is the emphasis in Mark 11:17 on *prayer* or on *the nations*? Prayer is the assumed activity at the Temple. That prayer would be offered to the God of Israel by "all nations" is the radical message of Jesus to that society. Non-Jewish ethnicities were condemned by the motifs of holiness and separateness. They were demonized by the fever of messianic nationalism.[200] The Jews did not want to be contaminated; they kept their distance from the nations.

In order to explain his actions when 'cleansing the temple' Jesus quotes Isaiah 56:7, "My house shall be called a house of prayer for all nations (*ethnos*)." The context of Christ's quote in Isaiah makes it clear that the emphasis was on the word "nations." Verse 6 reads, "The sons of *the stranger* (the foreigner) are to be brought in." Isaiah 56 and 57 envisions the postexilic return from Babylon. There are conflicts between those returning and those who had not left. The question is implied, "Who are the true people of God?" Isaiah's answer is that it could be anyone – even the foreigner.

The foreigner should not say that the Lord has separated him from His people (Isa. 56:3). Nor should the eunuch, formerly excluded from the temple, feel that he has no place (v. 4). Rather the Lord says, "to them I will give in My house and within My walls a place and a name better than that of sons and daughters" (v. 5). For God's house is *everyone's* house. God's embrace and acceptance is based on doing the will of God, not on ritualistic acceptance of codes of holiness. Verse 7 is a promise to the eunuch and the foreigner who have kept justice and done righteousness. "Even them I will bring to my holy mountain, and make them joyful in my house of prayer."

They are granted a place on God's holy mountain and their sacrifices are accepted.

Jesus' quote refers not only to Isaiah 56, but also to Jeremiah 7. There the prophet delivers a diatribe against the temple (v. 4). The phrase "den of thieves" or "cave of bandits" comes from Jeremiah's temple sermon – "one of the bitterest attacks on the temple stated in the Hebrew Bible."[201] Israelites were tolerating injustice toward the poor, the immigrants, and the foreigners (v. 6). God threatens to destroy His own house calling it a 'den of thieves' (v. 11). It was unthinkable to the Jewish mind that the temple would be destroyed. This was God's home. Would he destroy His own dwelling place or allow someone else to do so?

The problem at the temple was not simply that merchandising was going on. The buying and selling of sacrifices were necessary components of the sacrificial system established by the Torah.[202] Pilgrims had to acquire animals "without blemish" for sacrifice after the long arduous journey from a distant city. They must exchange money to pay the half-shekel temple tax. Most have assumed that the merchants were unjust - exploiting the poor and accruing profits for the priestly leaders at the expense of the pilgrims. Is this the problem Jesus addresses in the phrase "you have made it a cave of bandits"? According to Abrahams, "There is little evidence of abuse in the temple system."[203]

Jesus drives out the buyers and sellers. Was his primary concern the commercialism of the day and the exploitation of the poor? Or, was it the overwhelming of the courtyard with business that made it impossible to worship and pray - the one location where *Gentiles* should be able to find a place of acceptance before God and a sense of His presence in prayer? The business of "bandits" is not thievery in this case. Mark does not choose the Greek word *klepto* (from which we get our word kleptomaniac) speaking of one who steals in secret. Rather he uses the word *lestes* (cf. 14:48 and 15:27; found in Josephus 42 times and in the NT 15 times) which is used for bands of marauders and insurrectionists. These are people known as violent revolutionists who hide out in caves. The word is used to denote revolutionary groups opposed to the Roman occupation - the Zealots, for example, who would not tolerate and actually combated the presence of *Gentiles* in their Holy Land. Thus, the temple became a nationalistic front for armed revolution and terrorism and a repudiation of the Gentile presence.

When the scribes and chief priests heard the express wish of Jesus they sought to destroy him (Mark 13:18). They thought they were helping to usher in God's Kingdom, a mono-cultural reign. In reality, Jesus said they were no more than thieves, their deeds making the temple "a cave of militant operations."[204] In the light of this idea, the desolating sacrilege that Jesus announces in Mark 13:14 takes on a whole new perspective. These separatists were precipitating divine judgment. The temple had become an institutional symbol of nationalistic exclusivism. It must be cleansed and rescued before the inclusive kingdom vision of Jesus can go forward and bear fruit. Ironically here, impurity results from a zealous preoccupation with purity.[205] Wholeness could only come if the temple were what it was meant to be - a place where peoples from *all nations* join to worship. If this institution was opposed to that ideal then it must be destroyed and replaced by another temple, one not made with hands (Mark 14:58; 13:27). This work is Jesus' work but it is also the work of the disciple of Christ.

The fig tree was cursed and it died (Mark 13:21). Jesus then seems to completely change direction in launching a discussion about faith. He speaks of casting this mountain into the sea (v. 23). The only "mountain" in the context is the temple mount. Disciples are empowered do the transformational things that Jesus can do. They can heal the sick and cast out demons (3:15; 6:13). They can also transform fruitless institutions. They can say to this mountain "be removed and cast into the sea." Jesus curses the fig tree and gives His disciples power to "curse the mountain" - power to curse the unfruitful religious institution. Faith enables the believer to bring to pass the promise of multicultural worship.

"Whatever you ask for when you pray. . . it will be yours" (11:24) – outrageous though it seems. What is being sought here is a place of prayer for all. The desire of Christ becomes the desire of his followers. Many are warring against the vision. Mono-cultural worship centers that are exclusive are fruitless. This comes down not as a condemnation of past or present day Judaism, but as a challenge to the present day church. It is an appeal for a renewal of the prophetic hope envisioned by Isaiah and John the revelator. Worship's end-time reality will occur in the present time. A cave of banditry will yield to a house of prayer for all the nations.

The cleansing of the synagogue in Mark 2 parallels the cleansing of the temple. Each uses the language of casting out. The word *ballo*, 'cast out,' reminds us that this is a symbolic strike against the kingdom of Satan.[206] It is the word used in John's gospel when Jesus says, "now is the prince of this world cast down" (John 12:31) and when the revelator sees Satan hurled down to the earth (Rev. 12:9). Jesus casts the demons out of the synagogue as He casts the sellers and the buyers out of the temple. The Kingdom is breaking in, shattering the power of Satan with a healing, future-directed kingdom transformation. The temple is 'possessed' and Jesus performs an exorcism.[207] The future, God's ideal, should exist in the present. The culminating worship service that will last for all eternity should happen here and now. Leaders who prevent this from happening keep God's temple from bearing fruit. They must be cast out even as demons are.

Segregated churches are the spiritually barren temples of Christendom. Busy prosperous churches may be simply leafy, fruitless trees. They may have millions of dollars in assets and thousands of congregants. But, if their worship remains the kind of worship that Jesus disdained, a worship including only those who are like ourselves, we have missed out on the opportunity to demonstrate the transformational and reconciling power of the Kingdom of righteousness.

Conclusion

The homogeneity principle often rules our churches today as purity and holiness codes ruled the lives of first century Jews. The assumption that visitors are more likely to join a church when they are with others of their kind is widely held. Programs may be easier to develop for one kind of people. Monocultural worship services are still desirable to many. But Jesus called for an apocalypse of worship, the realization of an end-time, multicultural reality – a temple where Jew and Gentile (of every kind) could worship as one. Now, this means a church desegregated along lines of race, ethnicity, and culture, as well as socio-economic status - the destruction of the fruitless institutions of homogeneity and removal of the mountains of discrimination and bigotry. We are to bring this "present" to an end and bring the future, God's reality, to the present.

CHAPTER THREE

THE CONTROVERSY
(သ

Some say that it does not work.
Others say that it cannot be done.
What a number of people in the pews, pulpits,
denominational offices and seminary classes in the
United States are talking about is the possibility of
creating a truly multicultural Christian congregation.
Michael Hawn

Introduction

The topic of the multicultural church and the assimilation of people of various ethnic backgrounds into the life and ministry of the local church has increasingly become a focus of discussion, particularly in the past decade. For decades the church growth movement seemed to negate the possibility or likelihood of the multicultural church experiencing success since the research seemed to indicate that homogeneous churches were the viable and growing churches.

In this chapter the questions to be addressed are, "Why is eleven o'clock Sunday morning in America still the most segregated hour?" and "What can, or should be done, if anything, to change that reality?" What have Christian leaders and authors been saying? The issues are considered in five major sections:

(1) Can Multicultural Churches Flourish?

    a. The Unifying Factors

    b. The Homogeneous Unit Principle

(2) Should Multicultural Churches Be Encouraged?

    a. The Benefits of Multicultural Churches

    b. Cautions Regarding the Multicultural Church

(3) How Intentional Must the Church Be?

    a. Preparing a Local Church for Cultural Diversity

    b. Understanding Other Cultures

(4) The Vision to Be Embraced

    a. What is the Ideal?

    b. How Do We Get There?

(5) Is it Necessary?

    a. The Imperative of the Gospel

    b. The Spiritual Dimension.

(1) Can Multicultural Churches Flourish?

There has been much debate over the last few decades about the advantages and disadvantages of multicultural churches, as well as the likelihood of such churches growing and flourishing. Stephen Rhodes says, "One of the questions I am asked most frequently is 'Does it work?' People seem genuinely perplexed at the viability of a multicultural church. The question reflects less a sense of whether multicultural churches ought to exist, than whether, they can exist."[208] Michael Hawn puts the question in perspective:

> Some say that it does not work. Others say that it cannot be done. What a number of people in the pews, pulpits, denominational offices and seminary classes in the United States are talking about is the possibility of creating a truly multicultural Christian congregation. Some say that nothing more than tokenism can be accomplished by forcing together people who do not want to worship as one. Others say that in any attempt to form a culturally diverse congregation, one cultural group will always dominate, overwhelming any smaller group. Some are cynical about the possibility of creating multicultural churches and argue that Christian congregations grow best when they are most homogeneous and have a common worship style shared by all. Their thesis is that similarity produces growth – so why resist uniformity? Occasionally one also hears the complaint that the calls for multicultural congregations are nothing more than examples of 'political correctness' and therefore a passing fad pushed by a faction within the church.[209]

Despite the controversy, the cynic and the naysayer, many today are catching a glimpse of a vision of multicultural churches, seeing, as David Anderson notes, "African-

Americans, Caucasians, Koreans, Latinos, and Jewish believers all celebrating the grace of God, who created beautiful and amazing diversity within the human race."[210] Charles Foster asks, "Why are a growing number of congregations challenging the historic preference for cultural and racial homogeneity in congregational life?"[211] It can be said that in order for this kind of vision to come to fruition it must be from God. It runs contrary to decades, even centuries, of church history in America. Black historian C. Eric Lincoln states:

> To the mind of the Negro the segregated church is the rawest symbol of the white man's inability to practice the Christianity he has sought to sell to millions of non-whites around the world. It is difficult to forget that in order to be a Christian in America the Negro has been required either to organize new churches or denominations, or accept an uncomplimentary status in white churches where his presence is not desired.[212]

Many discourage the cultivation of such a vision. Leaders in church planting have suggested, "It can't be done. One of the cultures ultimately will have to become dominant and the others will die."[213] However, Anderson, who intentionally planted a multicultural congregation challenges the assumption. He asserts that those who are enjoying the ministry of a multicultural church testify that God has changed their view of the world to be more like Christ's, as they see value in others whose culture, skin and traditions are different from theirs. These churchgoers declare that they are not only tolerating one another, they are genuinely loving, laughing, and celebrating, together as they realize their unity in Christ.[214] Anderson suggests that it is foolish for American churches to remain divided when they can instead enjoy the symphony of a multicultural church. A church where whites, blacks, Latinos, and Asians come together under the skillful conducting of the Lord Jesus – "a symphonic chorus of masterful proportions."[215] He raises the question, "What would one title such an amazingly multicultural, multifaceted, multidimensional book of love?" and then answers, tongue in cheek, "Perhaps – the Church. This is," as he terms it, "the church's new groove."[216] At GGF, we often find ourselves saying, "This is a taste of heaven."

The Unifying Factors

Jeter and Allen comment on the changes in society and the unifying factors in the church that are effecting change within houses of worship:

> There was a time when cultures evolved in relative isolation. No more. In cities, and even in rural areas, we find different cultures living next to and among one another. One no longer has to go from one congregation to another to encounter multiple cultures. Today many pastors stand up to preach in congregations of once majority Anglo Americans, that are now of an entirely different look. The catch-all term is that

the church has become 'multicultural.' There are few places where the concerns of multiculturalism have come into more conflict than in communities of faith. Some churches have successfully mediated that conflict; most have not. Successful multicultural churches have strong magnetic and unifying factors that draw and hold large varieties of people together in community, churches in which one can see wealthy patrician bankers sitting comfortably in the same pew with recent immigrant laborers, and where butchers, bakers and candlestick makers pray together.[217]

These authors identify tradition as the "unifying factor" in Roman Catholic parishes. In Pentecostal gatherings it is often "experience," along with the powerful activity of the Holy Spirit.[218] The "stand against common oppression" has been a feature of homogeneous ethnic churches (particularly in the African-American church) for decades. It is now being touted as a mark of the multicultural church. Whatever other "unifying factors" we might come up with in our research of multicultural churches, it must be emphasized that the work of God's Spirit and a commitment to principles of Scripture must be seen as primary.

The unifying factor in many multicultural congregations is often viewed as a powerful, charismatic preacher/ leader. My own experience of larger multicultural churches in Charismatic circles is that they have been pastored by Caucasians, e.g. Jim Cymbala of Brooklyn Tabernacle, David Wilkerson of Times Square Church, Jack Hayford of Church on the Way. These are Pentecostal pastors whose expository preaching and preaching style apparently has appeal to people of color. One must realize however that they are uniquely gifted preachers who naturally attract a wide listening audience. The style of music in these churches, which crosses over from various contemporary styles to traditional, and to Black gospel also attracts a diverse constituency. A Pentecostal African-American pastor who has had some success, and certainly great concern to build a multicultural congregation, is David Ireland of Christ Tabernacle.

Jeter and Allen state, "Most mainstream Protestant churches have not had the success in becoming intentionally multicultural that the groups just mentioned *(i.e. Romans Catholics and Pentecostals)* have had. They seem to lack a binding magnetic factor or, if they have one, it has become less and less a part of their life together, or disagreement has arisen about its meaning."[219] John Calvin, the father of Reformed theology, for example, is hardly a unifying factor for Presbyterians today. Many do not appreciate the man or his doctrine. But then again, most do not know much about the man or understand his doctrine.

Exceptions among mainline churches seem to be for the most part multicultural churches pastored by African-Americans, e.g. James Forbes at Riverside Church in NYC, Alvin Jackson at National City Christian Church in Washington, DC, and

Cecil Williams at Glide Memorial United Methodist Church in San Francisco. Characteristically:

> They are all dynamic preachers who preach an inclusive gospel that appeals to people across cultural boundaries. The churches they serve appear to have an understanding of the gospel that embraces, even insists upon, people of various cultures relating positively in communities of support and witness to the kind of world they believe God wants and the ways that they believe God wants people to live together.

Jeter and Allen suggest that African-American preaching style is more appealing to European American people than European American preaching is to African American people. One might conclude that there is a need for Caucasian pastors to appreciate the positive elements of the African American preaching style and to learn to incorporate elements of that style into their own. The Pentecostal/Charismatic preacher may find an easier adjustment at this point due to their naturally more expressive style.

Peter Wagner suggests that when leadership changes, churches that have chosen to mix homogeneous units often fragment. The apparently successful ones frequently revert to two or more congregations meeting in the same facilities.[220] However recent transitions challenge this conclusion. It appears that Times Square Church has overcome this tendency with Carter Conlan leading the congregation to continued health and growth. Jack Hayford apparently has successfully handed over the reins to Dan Hicks.

James Cone introduced the idea of "black theology" which is a way of relating the gospel message conditioned by the black experience and thus is greatly concerned with issues of justice. The issue of justice is far too seldom addressed in the white church. The social concerns of one group differ from that of another. One author states that "until Christians truly understand the divergent voting patterns of black and white evangelicals (among other political realities) we will have no chance whatsoever of achieving genuine racial reconciliation. It makes a vivid marker of all that divides us."[221] Political views seem to represent a huge challenge to unity in the multicultural church. Anderson suggests that bringing whites and blacks together in multicultural ministry may represent the greatest challenge as they are the "opposite ends of the spectrum as the world sees it," what he calls "bookends."[222].

The presidential election of 2008 is the perfect illustration of this. Among African-Americans there was a tremendous natural support for the first candidate of color ever for the Presidency of the United States. Other minority groups were also supportive. This was a tremendously significant and truly historic event for a race that had faced such a long history of oppression and discrimination. It was seen as a victory in the long struggle for equality. White evangelicals however generally were concerned with this president's stand on certain social issues (abortion, homosexuality, marriage). Many of them felt his positions to be anti-Christian and anti-family. Certainly there were individuals in all ethnic groups who did not fit into the above generalizations. Opinions were so divergent that it was easy for one group to actually question the faith of the other or at least one's faithfulness to Scriptural principles.

It is quite evident that our unity cannot be based on political and social issues but instead must be grounded in the Holy Spirit. One must depend on the Spirit to develop tolerance, and an understanding of and even appreciation for the perspectives of others. Far to often we judge others and determine their spirituality on the issues that are of most consequence to us.

The above paragraphs highlight the key issue of leadership and the role that leaders play. Many feel that "minority persons, including pastors, are more skilled at relating to majority persons than the other way around."[223] Church historian Justo Gonzalez's words are telling, "I have had to deal with you, your language, your culture, your rules. I have no choice. You, on the other hand, have not had to deal with me."[224] This statement suggests a need for the white pastor to be sensitive to, and understanding of, the plight of minority persons and aware of how their life experiences might cause them to respond to certain statements. Once again we should note that many white pastors apparently have navigated these waters successfully.

A volume I discovered near the end of my research, *One Body, One Spirit* by George Yancey, reflected a similar concern to understand the dynamics of multicultural ministry. This volume summarized a research project funded by the Lilly Foundation. Based on surveys reflecting the perspectives of church leaders, Yancey identified seven key factors that led people to attend or to be assimilated into multicultural congregations. These factors included: inclusive worship, diverse leadership, an overarching goal, intentionality, personal skills, location and adaptability. The factors will be examined after addressing the controversy and the criticism of the Homogeneous Unit Principle (HUP). However, we cannot conclude this section without emphasizing once again, that beyond the "identifiable unifying factors," the work of the Spirit and a commitment to Scriptural principles must be seen as primary. These elements are indeed essential in bringing together a multicultural congregation.

The Homogeneous Unit Principle

One of the more lively debates in the religious field in contemporary America revolves around the question of integration or segregation in local churches. It has been generally conceded that it is easier for churches to develop solely around one category or class of people, or as McGavran puts it, "Men like to become Christians without crossing racial, linguistic, or class barriers."[225] However, while it might be easier, Wagner continues,

> while people might feel more comfortable in such churches, larger questions need to be raised: Is it right and good for Christians to intentionally group themselves into congregations that generally reflect the culture and life-style of just one kind of people? Can a culturally homogeneous church be justified in a pluralistic society?[226]

Wagner, who is the great proponent of the Homogeneous Unit Principle (HUP), suggests that if the goal of the church is making disciples, then it is necessary to find the most effective method of making disciples. He therefore stresses the pragmatic aspect of homogeneous unit congregations:

> Disciples are more readily made by people within their own homogeneous unit, and congregations develop into healthy communities when they concentrate on only one kind of people. Human group affiliation is a vital force that can and should be used by Christians in fulfilling the Great Commission. This innate sense of community should be seen in a positive light, and the church should address people in community, changing aspects of culture where necessary, but not disturbing community or culture when not required to do so by Christian principles.[227]

Yancey states it this way:

> Proponents of the church growth school argue that to
> accomplish growth it is vital to create churches where
> potential members of that church are comfortable
> and will eventually join the church. One of the ways
> of developing this comfort level is to target certain
> subcultures. . . . Multiracial churches, by their nature
> contain many different subcultures. . . These differ-
> ences create the theoretical possibility of conflict and
> an atmosphere that is uncomfortable for new church
> attendees. Church growth experts argue that to spend
> energy putting together a church of many different
> racial groups detracts from the church's main duty - to
> win as many souls as possible.[228]

McGavran first wrote on the subject of the HUP in 1936
in a volume entitled *Church Growth and Group Conversion*. A
second book, *The Bridges of God*, was even more influential
and might be viewed as the beginning of the modern Church
Growth Movement. Wagner, as the key disciple of McGavran,
popularized the HUP through a number of books in the late
seventies. He states that the HUP is by no means the only,
or even the most distinguishing, characteristic of the church
growth movement but, particularly here in America, it was by
far the most controversial element.[229]

Wagner first identifies the positive aspect of ethnicity
stating that ethnicity gives people a sense of identity - "the
comfort and security of belonging to a group called 'we.' "[230]
At the same time ethnicity can be said to be the root cause

of some of the greatest miseries of humanity (war, genocide, oppression, slavery, and injustice). Ethnicity can be viewed as a moral issue because it both unites and divides people. "Suppose it is true," Wagner conjectures, "that eleven o'clock on Sunday morning is the most segregated hour in America. The questions remain: Is that good or bad? Does the Christian ethic demand that congregations be characterized by a mixture of the ethnic groups present?"[231]

Wagner challenges the idea that integration is the be all and end all.[232] He suggests that in America integration means that eventually everyone will speak English and will look and act like the "dominant culture." He expresses the controversial idea that this may not be the best thing for ethnic minorities. However, just as Wagner criticizes those who make integration the ultimate goal, one might question his assumption that evangelism is the supreme purpose or goal of the Church. The question set forth in this discussion is, "Does the end (evangelism) justify the means (segregation)?"

Evangelism, the salvation of lost souls, is often held up as the priority of the church. In the Scriptures worship is viewed time and again as an activity of the nations (particularly in Psalms and in Revelation). Could it be that the goal of evangelism should be and must be subjugated to the primary goal of worship in the church – that worship of the living Lord is to take precedence over evangelism? If worship is seen as even a greater priority than evangelism, then this matter of "efficiency" in evangelism becomes secondary to the goal of the nations worshiping their Creator. Evangelism is better viewed as the natural outflow of a people that together magnify and lift up the name of the Lord. In worship the Name of the Lord is exalted in the congregation and in evangelism that exalting of His Name is carried out into the marketplace.

Is it not possible that when the Spirit of the Lord is released in the worship of His people that He breaks down the barriers that divide men resulting in an ingathering of lost men and women into His Church? That certainly seems to be the message of Pentecost as it was the story of the Azusa Street revival of 1906. At Pentecost it was prophesying, that is, "declaring in our own tongues the wonderful works of God" (Acts 2:11) which led to an ingathering from the nations. At Azusa Street, in a day when the racial lines in America were much more distinct than they are today, the Spirit of God overturned all the natural divisions and brought blacks and whites together in an obviously miraculous expression of unity.

McGavran, in providing a rational for the HUP, acknowledges, "To me cultural diversity between countries was a nuisance, but cultural diversity within a country was simply an evil to be overcome." He confesses his cultural bias, "I had no thought of excluding anyone from any church but I did unconsciously assume that the best thing that could happen to Black, White, Chicano, etc., was that they all would eventually come to the White, Anglo-Saxon, Protestant church and learn to do things the way that I felt was most proper."[233] Today McGavran feels that this kind of inclusion of ethnicities in the local church, where they are required to conform to a dominant culture, would be detrimental to their spiritual life.

The point is valid. Do we want ethnicities to surrender their uniqueness whether in language or in culture? Some see cultural diversity within churches as an "evil to overcome" as they mistakenly equate "sameness" with "unity." Yancey says,

> Cultural pluralism questions the value of integration itself. They argue that in the rush to integrate members of multiple races we will allow the power of the dominant race to overwhelm the integrity of minority cultures . . . Advocates for racial minorities argue that this philosophy denigrates the culture . . . and implies that European American culture is superior. This philosophy of cultural pluralism mandates that the cultures of minority groups are to be respected and maintained in as pure a form as possible. Its proponents argue that the value of racial minority cultures is equal to the value of European American culture and to force racial minorities to accept a Euro-centric Christianity is sin.[234]

The reason that ethnicity has become a problem for Christian social ethicists, Wagner insists, is the "undeniable fact that most Christian congregations, whether they ought to be or not, are culturally homogeneous. Even in pluralistic societies where different groups of people live closely together and speak mutually intelligible languages, churches seem to develop in 'homogeneous units.' "[235] Missiological research, as well as sociological research, bears out the fact that in America most Christians "meet together for worship and fellowship within the basic sociological groupings into which they were born."[236] Wagner goes one step further in saying that in various countries and cultures around the world, the church "seems to develop most vigorously when it is allowed or even encouraged to grow in specific homogeneous groups rather than forced to include different groups."[237]

Wagner observes, "The HUP applies chiefly, not on the denominational level, but on the congregational level where the fellowship dimension of church life is prominent."[238] He suggests that in a large church there may be a broadly heterogeneous group but it is often subdivided internally into several homogeneous units.[239] He asks three significant questions of those churches which appear to be successfully heterogeneous.

First, "Is the heterogeneity illusory?" Circle Church in Chicago appeared to be multicultural but was made up of Asian, black, and white "intellectuals." In its own way, it was a homogeneous assembly despite the color differences. Interestingly enough, this assumed model of a "multicultural church" later experienced a split along racial lines. When one ethnicity enjoys the worship and preaching style of another ethnic group they may assimilate to the norm doing little to influence, impact, or change that style. There are some blacks, for example, who prefer more punctual, "dignified" liturgical worship and thus may lean toward what may seem to be more typical of a Caucasian worship experience. In such situations, where minority members simply assimilate to existing styles, one may ask if the result is truly a multicultural church.

Secondly, "Is the heterogeneity transitory?" If the neighborhood is in transition it is very likely that the heterogeneity of the church will not endure. Once the "minority" group reaches a majority of the church membership, the transformation may become a rapid one, as the formerly dominant ethnicity begins to feel uncomfortable with their loss of power and exits. One group is phasing out while another is replacing it.

Lastly, "Is the heterogeneous church growing?" Wagner acknowledges that there are mature Christians who understand "oneness in Christ" and thus embrace coexistance with those of other ethnicities. But is it possible for them to reach the unchurched and unsaved, those who do not understand the concept of Christian unity? Unchurched people presumably know nothing of "oneness in Christ," as Christians do, and thus "lack the spiritual motivation that Christians might have for welcoming close associations with people of other homogeneous units."[240] The HUP is concerned with church growth as well as with church survival. Wagner says that for optimum conditions of growth, the composition of a congregation should be compatible with the needs for social companionship felt by the unchurched people in the community.

He contends, with regard to this issue of church growth and heterogeneity, "although I do not have empirical evidence to confirm it, my impression is that if any truly heterogeneous churches are growing in America, they are the exception to the general rule."[241] Typically those that are growing, he says, have an exceptional leader. Frequently, in this type of church, the philosophy of ministry places "heavy emphasis on the celebration or worship service" with church attendees being "little more than weekly spectators, and no more problems arise in mixing homogeneous units in that style of worship than mixing them in a baseball stadium. If fellowship groups do develop the problems will become more acute."[242]

However, after twenty years as a pastor engaging in multicultural church life, I must disagree. At GGF the celebration or worship service is central. However, people stay long after the celebration is over conversing in the lobby and building relationships. Our fellowship groups and ministry teams are all integrated and are constantly bringing people into vital relationships with one another across ethnic lines. We place a high value on fellowship and relationships that take us outside our natural circle of friends. While there may be challenges it is certainly working and congregants celebrate along with me the joy of expanded perspectives.

Despite his commitment to the HUP, Wagner does acknowledge that "what is cannot be taken as what ought to be."[243] He concludes, "Just because Christian churches do tend to be culturally homogeneous and just because they do seem to maintain more growth and vitality when they remain as such does not, of course, lead to the conclusion that they should be homogeneous."[244] He offers options:

> Christians, therefore, are free to group themselves in churches in whatever way they wish along homogeneous or heterogeneous lines. Both are good Christian options, but the decision should be made intelligently, and the consequences of each option weighed. If the option of crossing homogeneous unit lines and mixing two or more different groups in the congregation is chosen, the positive effect is that Christians will feel very good about their success in breaking through racial or class barriers. They will also be enriched by the interaction with and exposure to people of other cultures. However . . . the evangelistic potential of the church will be seriously curtailed.[245]

The focus on evangelism to the exclusion of "what ought to be" should not be left unchallenged.

This assumption, that the evangelistic potential of a church will be curtailed if it becomes multicultural, needs to be challenged. Yancey presents evidence to the contrary. It has been this author's experience that this is a fallacious assumption. Since 1980 (when GGF averaged about 150 in attendance), the church has seen steady growth, approximately doubling in size each decade since then. This growth was unhindered and, in fact, promoted by the increasing diversity. One of the most compelling reasons people cited for visiting GGF, and certainly, an undeniable reason they choose to stay, was because of its diversity. In Gracepoint's experience, diversity has not been a detriment but rather an aid to evangelism. Harmony and demonstrated love in a diverse community is one of the most convincing and persuasive proofs of the validity of the gospel. In a diverse and fragmented society it appears that people are seeking for ways to connect across ethnic lines. A byword of the Gen-Xer is relationship or connectedness. What better place for it to happen than in the church?

Throughout his book Wagner continues to defend the practical use and Biblical underpinnings of the HUP. He firmly believes that this principle does not encourage discriminatory practices but instead is one that protects and ensures the continuance of various cultural expressions in a most meaningful dimension of life – that of worship. Yancey sums up another aspect of the dialogue:

> Since the church is an important center of the culture of many racial minority groups, cultural pluralists are generally skeptical of multiracial churches. . . . The

development of black theology has supported the idea of maintaining distinct African American congregations and liberation theology has supported the value of maintaining the uniqueness of Latino American congregations. Such theologies regard preventing the loss of black and Latino culture as a priority for minority Christians. While cultural pluralists may not directly attack the worth of multicultural churches, their desire for multiracial churches is low since such churches may lead to the assimilation of minority cultures by the majority group.[246]

These assumptions will be challenged by asking and answering the next question.

(2) Should Multicultural Churches Be Encouraged?

John Perkins critically states, "Something is wrong at the root of American evangelicalism. I believe we have lost the focus of the gospel – God's reconciling power, which is unique to Christianity – and have substituted church growth. We have learned to reproduce the church without the message. It is no longer a message that transforms."[247] Henry Wilson adds, "Christians and churches should welcome the flowering of multiculturalism in North America as an opportunity to reclaim their authentic nature as Pentecost Christians."[248] Jurgen Moltmann argues that the Christian church, if it is to be authentic, must be heterogeneous. According to him, a racial church or class church is "heathenish and heretical."[249] To be an effective witness of reconciliation to the world, the church must demonstrate to those around it that internally it has done the job of reconciling like and unlike. The church must consist "of the educated and the uneducated, of the black and white, of the high and the low."[250] Churches are at their best, Moltmann believes, when they contradict the natural groupings of human beings, and they do poorly when they conform to such groupings.

John Stott suggests that mixed congregations are stronger in their witness. "The more mixed the congregation is, especially in 'class' and 'color,' the greater its opportunity to demonstrate the power of Christ."[251] The breakdown of the "wall of hostility" between Jew and Gentile, between slaves and masters, in the first century, was a miracle of God. "So is the overcoming of the barriers of race and rank today," Stott insists.[252] Ephesians provides the rationale for the heterogeneous church. The church must channel the unifying power of Christ wherever "the hostilities of nation, race, culture, religiousness, class, are destroying the unity of God's creation. Do not churches composed of just one kind of people tend to deepen those worldly separations rather than bring the uniting reconciling power of Christ to bear in such a way that these worldly barriers collapse?"[253]

These authors rightly abhor racial and class prejudice on display in the church. The Great Commandment is the impetus, inspiration, and challenge to the church to spearhead the reconciliation of various peoples to one another. The effectiveness of the church's ministry of reconciliation in the world is conditional upon its achieving a tangible and visible unity within the church. This unity can only be manifested in the local church when cross-cultural relationships are developed. These authors would all agree that the HUP is a threat to that unity and to the ministry of reconciliation. Thus the attempt to encourage growth in the church according to the HUP is seen as "immoral."

In McGavran's defence, he did not come to his conclusions regarding the HUP quickly or easily. Rather than seeing the HUP as "heathen and heretical," he sees it as "a dynamic to be harnessed for the effective fulfillment of the Great Commission."[254] On the mission field, he observed the tendency for groups of people to move, to change and to convert as a body rather than as individuals. This concept may be difficult for Westerners, socialized to value individualism, to grasp. The HUP can however, be a great aid to evangelization in "collective cultures."

Ralph Winter, a colleague of McGavran, says, "people blindness" and a lack of sensitivity to cultures can cause a Christian to "confuse the legitimate desire for church unity with the illegitimate goal of uniformity." Furthermore, "Christian unity cannot be healthy if it infringes on Christian liberty."[255] Although he recognizes that, "Inclusiveness is intrinsic and not accidental to the nature of the church,"[256] he suggests that pressure for any people group to conform to cultural norms in the name of Christianity is a violation of Christian liberty.

Christian liberty relates, for the most part, to those things that may be termed nonessentials. Foods or "meats," even those sacrificed to idols, according to Paul, are in this category of nonessentials (1 Corinthians 8). One is no better off if he abstains and no worse off if he partakes (v. 8) because the idol has no effect on the meat. Many matters of culture fall into this category of the non-essentials. Who are we, the apostle asks, that we should "judge someone else's servant?" (Rom. 14:4). Therefore it is imperative that we give people the freedom to hold onto cultural traditions that do not really interfere with their practice of Christianity and worship and may even enhance it in some way, at least for them. In the same way it is wrong for us to force people to conform to our preferred cultural practices when these practices are not essential to following after the Lord Jesus.

Padilla and Escobar, colleagues from Latin America, are also dissatisfied with, critical of, and opposed to the HUP calling it "culture Christianity." They characterize this principle as squeezing the church into the mold of the world with racial and class segregation. Padilla comments, "We are told that race prejudice 'can be understood and should be made an aid to Christianization.' No amount of exegetical maneuvering can ever bring this approach in line with the explicit teaching of the New Testament regarding the unity of men in the body of Christ."[257] The Christian church may be the only place left where encounter, acceptance, and coexistence can be modeled to society at large. Escobar states, "To perpetuate segregation for the sake of numerical growth, arguing that segregated churches grow faster, is for me yielding to the sinfulness of society." He then asks, "Is this really the church of Jesus Christ?"[258]

Reinhold Niebuhr, as far back as 1929, traced the origin of many denominations to racial or cultural, rather than religious or doctrinal, reasons. He accused these religious denominations of conformity to the order of social classes and says they demonstrated the "invasion of the church by the principle of caste."[259] He passed severe judgment on such denominationalism and called the development of denominations the "ethical failure of the divided church." [260] The founding of the General Council of the Assemblies of God in 1914, for example, has been attributed to a desire, on the part of some, for racial segregation from the Church of God, led by a black preacher by the name of Charles Mason.[261] Prior to the denominational split, Mason had ordained dozens of white ministers. That was, at the time, an extraordinary breakthrough in race relations. Apparently that revolution could not be tolerated for very long.

Randy Woodley addresses the need of this day in America:

> As neighborhoods become more integrated and diverse, the standards of homogeneity will not work. In fact, this Church will have the opposite effect from the one it desires. As the population becomes more diversified, our temptation will be to reinforce the ghetto mentality of homogeneity rather than to embrace and celebrate diversity. . . . Monocultural churches that live by the philosophy of 'like draws like' instead of healing the wounds of society, and regardless of what color 'like' happens to be, will serve to deepen the wounds and create more mistrust. As each ethnic group continues to gain exposure, we will experience more racial crises, yet have greater opportunities as well for cross-cultural friendships and marriages. These inevitable partnerships are, and will continue to be, a learning experience and celebration of God's great diversity among us. Wouldn't it be strange for people to have friendships and marriages and children that celebrate God's diversity, yet be unable to find churches where the very fabric of their being is not accepted? Where will those from such culturally diverse backgrounds go for godly counsel? What will it take for the monocultural Church of today to ready herself for the awaiting multicultural world?[262]

Gallagher suggests desegregation of churches as a solution to the blight of racism. He advocates interracial churches and calls for ministers from different groups to work side by side. He argues, "there is nothing but human inertia and a certain unreasoning fear of the unfamiliar to stand in the way of our making every congregation in this nation a cross section of the family of God."[263]

Pope calls the church the most segregated institution in American society. This is a result, he says, "of a deficiency in their understanding of the true nature and purpose of the church."[264] He suggests that, for blacks, being separate is only preferable to being inferior in white congregations. While Henry Wilson provides a historical perspective that acknowledges the place of monocultural churches, he develops the case for moving beyond these:

> Social and historical circumstances led several earlier immigration communities to succumb to the temptation of being endogamous Christians in their new environment of North America. The preservation of race, language, and other ethnic and cultural particularities in an alien land justified such an expression. The transitory localized nature of Christianity has become the norm, rather than the expression of Pentecostal Christianity. However, the increased multiculturalism in the US and around the world now makes it possible for churches to reclaim and to live out the Pentecost nature of Christianity in a much more intentional way, opening themselves to the pluralism of the communities already existing in the neighborhood. Embracing multiculturalism is not an option for Christians but a mandate. It is a call for discarding a false notion of Christian community, despite its long-cherished legacy.[265]

These authors make it clear that a homogeneous church, which is a divided church, will miss out on some of the greatest opportunities for witness and ministry in this generation.

Finally, the issue of church growth is addressed by Yancey's study. Based on analysis of his data, Yancey found that multicultural churches were actually more likely to have grown during his year long study than monoracial churches (66.1 percent to 57.1 percent). He concludes:

> Americans who have been socialized with only members of their own race are becoming less common. . . . If creating a comfortable environment is what is important to church growth, then multiracial churches should be more likely to grow than monoracial churches. . . . This evidence shows that the church growth argument is flawed. Churches that are not based on a single racial culture are more likely to grow than monoracial churches, probably through their ability to attract Americans who are very comfortable with multiracial social settings.[266]

Yancey is, at least in part, agreeing with the church growth argument which made the point that people will attend church where they are most comfortable. Since the ethnic composition of society has dramatically changed, many people are more likely to be comfortable with the multicultural church today than with the segregated church. This is particularly true of the younger generations. Yancey's study also addresses the myth that there is more conflict and thus less stability in multiracial churches. His conclusion from the research data was that multiracial churches "are no more likely to experience conflict than monoracial churches. . . . Concerns about the instability of multiracial churches, relative to monoracial churches, are not supported by empirical data."[267]

The Benefits of Multicultural Churches

Are there benefits to being part of a multicultural congregation? Various writers applaud the merits of the multicultural church. Manuel Ortiz says,

> I believe we limit the greatness of our Lord when we know God only as a local God who speaks our language and understands our conditions alone. The multiethnic church provides us with a more comprehensive understanding of the Scriptures. It takes away our haughtiness – our belief that we are more important and more knowledgeable than anyone else. It teaches us to learn the Word in more depth because the insights of others help us to see things that our blinders shut out before. It tells us that we need each other (1 Cor. 12:12-27) . . . the Great Commission is expressed through the testimonies of individuals with many accents . . .[268]

Foster contends that for some congregations racial and cultural differences were not stumbling blocks to their experience of community; rather they became "gifts and resources in forming community."[269]

Jeter and Allen list the benefits of multiculturalism in the church as the following:

- It broadens and deepens our own limited and circumscribed experience, as individuals and as community . . .
- It prepares us for more effective and satisfying living in the real world of the new millennium as we better understand our own culture and better relate to others . . .
- It moves us toward that time when we shall all gather before the throne of grace to share in the joys of God together.[270]

Yancey sees several advantages that multiracial churches enjoy: 1) an increased ability to reach multicultural communities (which are becoming the norm in our society); 2) an increased ability to promote racial reconciliation; 3) a tangible demonstration of racial unity which serves as a witness to the power of the gospel; 4) a demonstration of simple obedience to the Word of God. He says, "It can be argued that segregated churches generally reflect the culture of their racial group more than a Christian culture."[271]

Patty Lane likewise expresses support for the concept of the multicultural congregation:

From my experience I know that there is a profound witness given when people from great diversity come together through the power and love of God. I have seen entire communities transformed when someone from a victimized or terrorized group has reached out to their cultural enemies, or when one from a warring nation repents publicly to those who have been attacked. His asking for forgiveness, not for his personal wrongdoings but for those of his countrymen, seems to release the power of God to break down barriers and begin a healing process. Without diversity we would not see God work in the human heart in this mighty and miraculous way.[272]

In the words of Gonzalez, "To say the church is 'catholic' means that it includes within itself a variety of perspectives. To say that it is 'one' means that such multiplicity, rather than dividing it, brings it closer together."[273] Just as God brought together a man and a woman with two very different perspectives in the institution of marriage, the closest human relationship, it is clear that He wants men to have more than one (cultural) perspective in the church, the institution He has created and through which He accomplishes His work in the world today. Henry Wilson speaks of those immigrating to our shores:

If not included already, the Christian newcomers in the neighborhood . . . will be able to enrich historical churches in North America with their experience, articulation, and practice of the Christian faith, shaped by their worldviews and cultural heritages. Their experience of the divine, gained through means of their own cultures, and their spirituality and religiosity, shaped by their cultural perspectives are equally as valuable as the experiences and religiosities of other Christians.[274]

Michael Hawn states that a "danger of culturally uniform worship is that an ethnocentric perspective limits one's worldview."[275] Although he acknowledges that worship in that setting may be a "refuge" from the world, it runs the risk of excluding those who are different. If and when a congregation moves from cultural uniformity toward a "cultural partnership," he says, members will develop a greater self-consciousness about their own personal bias and thus be more open to the perspective of others. "A healthy bias is a posture of inclusion."[276] Eric Law writes, "Inclusion is a discipline of extending our boundary to take into consideration another's needs, interests, experience, and perspective, which will lead to clearer understanding of ourselves and others, fuller description of the issue at hand, and possibly a newly negotiated boundary of the community to which we belong."[277] These words echo the apostle's admonition to "look not to our own interests but to the interests of others" (Phil. 2:4).

Multicultural communities are needed in the church for many reasons including: the dismantling of prejudices; enabling cultural synthesis; enriching life; strengthening our witness; advocating for justice; producing Christian education and worship resources with due attention to cultural diversities; and developing cross-cultural ministerial formation programs.[278] Hawn asserts:

> Culturally conscious worship leads congregations toward a community that reflects the 'one new humanity' presented in Ephesians 2. This new humanity values the dignity and perspective of each person. Worship that emanates from this diverse body of believers is greater than the sum of its parts. The mosaic of a culturally diverse congregation in worship reflects the face of God from whom all cultures come.[279]

While the "fear is that only racial minorities will have to change to accommodate white Americans," the truth is that "interracial interaction gives racial minorities an opportunity to influence majority group members as well. . . . whites who attend churches where blacks also attend are more likely to have sympathetic attitudes toward the social and political interests of blacks than whites who attend churches where there are no blacks."[280] This has certainly been the experience at GGF due to the interaction of ethnicities. When racial issues were dealt with openly and honestly in small groups it brought new understanding to all participants of the plight of the "other" as well as a recognition that there are certain shared experiences that cross racial lines. The multicultural congregation provides an opportunity for spiritual growth, for "denial of self," for understanding and for developing an "other-orientation." Together the races can be stronger than they would be alone.

Cautions Regarding the Multicultural Church

A resistance to the multicultural church, on the other hand, has come from "the fear - no the reality - that less powerful cultures will be swallowed up by more powerful ones."[281] Wilson comments, "Supporters of multiculturalism argue that cultural homogenization is in fact cultural hegemony (domination). They point out that American unity is maintained at the expense of diversity."[282] Patty Lane says, "For many in the United States, the talk of assimilation (the process of cultural values and behaviors becoming like that of another culture's) is anathema. For others, generally from the dominant culture, to resist assimilation seems ludicrous," but "from a cultural perspective assimilation represents the death of one's heritage."[283] Within the next century it is projected that half of the world's languages will disappear.[284] In reaction to this loss of language and of culture in our quest for modern "sameness," there is certainly legitimate reason to seek to maintain and even to restore cultures and languages that are being lost.

This is one reason that Wagner gives for supporting the HUP. This principle, rather than demanding conformance to a dominant culture, allows for the diverse culture to be preserved and protected in one of the most important spheres, the place of worship. His concern is that when the minority group joins a church with a dominant culture it will inevitably be engulfed and destroyed. Thus he counters the criticism that the HUP is racist by implying that, in fact, the HUP is truly supportive of and defending racial and ethnic diversity.

Foster warns us of the difficulties of being part of a multi-cultural body:

> Daily encounters with the differences that exist among the people of these congregations provide a persistent confrontation with the depths of the racism in the church and society and the ethnocentrism that exists in almost all of us. . . . It is not easy to give up generations of practice of referring to people with stereotypical names or descriptions. It is difficult to change patterns of deference and expectations of privilege deeply embedded in our cultural bones."[285]

He goes on to speak of how the distinctiveness of our own cultural heritage is deeply rooted. This affects everything from how we smell the food at the covered dish dinner to how we decorate the sanctuary, to what musical sounds are pleasing and which ones are discordant or irreverent. "These differences extend to communication patterns which influence the way they understand the relationships of children and adults and leaders and followers, how decisions are made, and the ways in which the mysteries of God are acknowledged and practiced."[286] He then adds that becoming a part of a multicultural congregation "requires becoming conscious of that which is unconscious, of doing that which seems unnatural."[287]

The biggest problem in multicultural relationships, Lane says, is "misattribution." This is "attributing meaning or motive to someone's behavior based upon one's own culture or experience."[288] This occurs because our own cultural beliefs are so ingrained in us that they appear to be "common sense." They often evoke an "instant emotional response."[289] Lane goes on to give the following advice in order to avoid misattribution:

> 1) Learn about your own culture's values and behaviors. 2) Learn about the specific culture with which you are working. 3) Learn to check things out by asking a "cultural coach," that is, someone from that culture who will help you understand the culture and give you guidance on specific issues. 4) Learn ways to talk about culture and its impact on your relationships with your friends from other cultures. 5) Learn to ask yourself, "On what am I basing my feelings and thoughts about this relationship?" Make sure you are not basing them on a misattribution.[290]

Lane further expounds,

> It is easy to believe that one's culture is the best – because it works so well for you. . . . The truth is that all cultures are equal in their ability to work for the people of that culture. Problems arise, however, when people from different cultures enter into relationship

with each other and the beliefs long taken for granted are no longer shared.[291]

As cultures collide people may respond with xenophobia (fear of another culture), ethnocentrism (the belief that one's culture is superior to others), forced assimilation (making others conform to our culture) or segregation (keeping the cultures separate).

The challenge for the church is to respond with acceptance (the idea that all cultures are equal and should be respected) and even more so, celebration (this goes beyond tolerating to embracing and valuing). "Celebration is characterized by valuing other cultures because God created us as cultural beings and values diversity in all of creation. This attitude appreciates mutuality in relationships and the desire for multicultural experiences and relationships."[292] This means that in a church setting newcomers will be embraced and room will be found for their gifts and talents. There is recognition that no one culture has a corner on truth or spirituality.

The church must learn to appreciate diverse cultures, yet it must also confront certain cultural beliefs and rituals since that are sinful. In the past, Indian culture endorsed the practice of burning a wife alive on her husband's grave. Today within various cultures there are those who see no problem with wife beating. Jeter and Allen state:

> Realizing the positive qualities of multiculturalism can lead to automatic uncritical approval of anything from another, generally non-Western, non-European culture. . . . Rushing to embrace another culture may leave one in an awkward position of embracing values that go against the flow of the gospel. A true Christian multiculturalism would suggest that everyone has to change and that we are in error when we overemphasize our culture of origin to the exclusion of the transcending Christ.[293]

Rituals and beliefs can be positive, neutral or sinful. In the multicultural church there must be an evaluation and "classification" of these practices. Some aspects of culture can indeed be celebrated. Others need to be challenged and still others need to be confronted and corrected in accordance with the Word of God. The danger is that we are apt to judge another's culture before we have objectively looked at practices within our own culture. One is to remove the log in his eye before pointing out the splinter in someone else's.

(3) How Intentional Must The Church Be?

There is certainly a difference of opinion as to whether or not one must be intentional in building a multicultural congregation. For Yancey "intentionality" is a key factor in bringing into being a multicultural congregation. Although some pastors feel that multiracial churches have "just happened," Yancey strongly disagrees. He is adamant that preserving a multiracial mix is impossible without intentional efforts on the part of the church leadership. When one examines his list of seven factors that promote a multiracial congregation several, if not all, of them can be tied to this one - intentionality. The other six he lists are inclusive worship, diverse leadership, an overarching goal, personal skills, location and adaptability.

Jim Cymbala, pastor of the well-known Brooklyn Tabernacle, espouses a different perspective. When asked in an informal conversation if he had done anything intentional to grow a multicultural congregation, he was adamant that he had not. When asked if leaders should be sought that reflect the cultural diversity of the church he also expressed opposition to that idea. He stated simply that "a man's gifts and calling will make room for his ministry" and that God would provide the leaders necessary to oversee and grow the congregation.[294] Author and editor Dean Merrill, who was part of the conversation, shared his personal observation of Cymbala's relational style: "You and Carol, however, have always been very open to people of color in positions of leadership." Cymbala's response was, "When I played basketball for the University of Rhode Island I didn't care what color the player was as long as he could put the ball in the basket." His experience in the athletic arena had obviously helped to prepare him to work with and accept people of color in the church. His comments point out the danger of trying to orchestrate through human effort what can only be done by the Spirit of God. Cymbala is quoted by Peart as saying:

> As we experience God through the power of the Holy Spirit, we will look at the world the way God looks at the world. When we emphasize our race or culture, we are then glorifying an accident of our birth. You did not choose to be black, white, American, et cetera. Others are boasting in the different colors of their skin or the countries they were born in. We need to be the spiritual people that God wants us to be, which will then transcend mere culture and color. We need to relate to people not after their flesh but after their spirit. The hearts of all people are the same and the truly spiritual ministry can relate and speak into the hearts of them all.[295]

Although Cymbala may not see himself as intentional in the way many of us would define or think of that term, a view of his church's facility reflects a multicultural sensitivity. When touring the new facility of the Brooklyn Tabernacle, it is obvious, as one enters the lobby area and views the massive main stairwell, that thought has been given to creating an environment where people of color, as well as whites, would be comfortable and feel welcome. Huge murals cover the walls. These portray slaves worshiping and evangelist Aimee Semple McPherson's daughter being baptized in a river surrounded by a crowd of African-American congregants. (McPherson was well ahead of her time in breaking down the barriers of racism in the church.) Another mural depicts the preaching of D. L. Moody to what was primarily a white crowd. These murals, chosen by Cymbala, demonstrate the heart of a pastor receptive of people of all ethnicities. The music of the Brooklyn Tabernacle, without a doubt, has a black gospel flavor to it so that the atmosphere of this great church is conducive to the entrance of blacks and other minorities. Certainly the message of the Tabernacle is one of love and acceptance of all and one that teaches the value of all persons before God.

Yancey describes the multiracial church with these words:

> With rare exceptions, multiracial churches generally are not merely Eurocentric churches that have somehow managed to attract racial minorities. For the most part racial minorities do not go to churches that totally ignore their cultural concerns. Multiracial churches that tend to be successful are churches that attempt to meet the needs of members of all races. In this way multiracial churches are not simply bastions of European American culture, but tend to be a mixture of different racial cultures.[296]

Several authors go to great extent to illustrate the intentional efforts of churches and church leaders to attract minorities or to conserve gains from other ethnicities whereas Cymbala implies that such intentionality is unnecessary where the Spirit of God is at work. He insists that the work of the Spirit makes the components that bring about integration very natural and suggests that the elements that resist integration are done away with as the Spirit is given control. This is not to suggest that monoracial churches are void of the Spirit. Even where the Spirit is moving in power, Christians can be blind to some of His desires and unheeding of certain of His demands.

There is need for deliberate and purposeful action in order to be obedient to His will and directives. It seems entirely appropriate, in this author's mind, to use the words "planned, purposeful, deliberate and intentional" when speaking of action to promote and encourage multicultural churches in the light of man's (including the Christian's) natural tendency to remain with those who are most like us. These words appear to be descriptive of many of the features of Brooklyn Tabernacle.

One might also propose that human efforts to attain a multicultural congregation may fail miserably if the direction of His Spirit and the touch of God on those endeavors is missing. Intentional efforts at realizing this objective may seem to be contrived and sometimes justifiably criticized as man-made or "clever schemes." In case studies done by Hawn, the need for intentionality in developing multicultural congregations is repeatedly stated. The following paragraphs give us a few examples as well as pieces of our story at Gracepoint. (If any of you would like to share your own story of multicultural church life and factors that led to diversity in your setting please email me at <u>pastorcarl@gracepointgospel.org</u>).

All Nations United Methodist Church in Plano, Texas was planted with the express intention of being a multicultural congregation. The congregation echoes its motto, "Christian by faith, diverse by design" often during worship, the congregants conveying this motto with passion.[297] The name of the church signifies the intention of the founding pastor, Dr. Clara Reed. Prayer and worship are key elements of not only the Sunday worship but of every meeting in the church. Hawn notes, "Nurturing diversity is a communal spiritual discipline for many members."[298] One of its distinctive features is its conscious attempt to ensure representative ethnic diversity in all of its leadership, educational, and serving roles. The church does not seem to "follow the usual pattern of most racially and ethnically homogeneous mainline congregations. In every aspect of its administrative and organizational life, All Nations has a diversity of people involved. . . . The leadership reflects the congregation's differences in culture, background, and class."[299] Four lay preachers also reflect the diversity of the church.

There are a variety of worship styles offered and the worship is intentionally inclusive. Even the worship team is chosen to model diversity with two Anglos and two African-Americans, two women and two men leading each week. A conscious desire to attract Hispanics to the church is obvious in the welcome and closing often being given in Spanish and in the use of Spanish creeds and hymns in worship. Members of the congregation have expressed

> an uninformed sense of search or calling for this type of congregational life and mission - a longing that remained unarticulated until they came to All Nations. To others, coming to All Nations was a homecoming, although 'home' was a place they had never seen before . . . Some congregants have speculated that those who have tasted of a multicultural reality may continue to thirst for it.

A sense of community and communal ownership of ministry characterize the church. The ritual of the "passing of the peace" lasts for at least ten minutes in the Sunday morning service encouraging a greater depth of fellowship than many congregations would enjoy.

There can be danger that human effort to promote diversity run contrary to the work of the Spirit and thus run amuck. If leaders are chosen simply for the sake of diversity or to "fill quotas," the efforts may be counterproductive. Spiritual leaders must fulfill spiritual qualifications, demonstrate a level of spiritual maturity and be called of God to the office or responsibility. There must be a confidence that the Holy Spirit will lead people into the offices and tasks that need to be filled within the body. The Spirit of God will accomplish what men can only hope to achieve.

At Gracepoint we did not start out with intentional efforts to bring about diversity. It was after the diversity began to be evident that we started to ask the questions of how we should respond to it, what could we do to encourage it, to be sensitive to the concerns of other cultures, etc. We did realize that certain decisions we had previously made had encouraged the diversity. A key staff person contributing to diversity was certainly our minister of music. The Lord brought Richard Smith, a gifted African-American musician, keyboard player and songwriter to our congregation early on. His ability to introduce and lead in a variety of music styles enabled us to enjoy black gospel music without moving exclusively in that direction. White members of the congregation were able to worship in a way that they were accustomed to while also learning to appreciate a different cultural approach to worship.

Certainly Pastor Cymbala's sense that a man's gifts and calling will make room for his ministry is Biblical and cannot be contested. However, one must ensure that there is openness on the part of the current leadership and a willingness to receive any one (of any color) that the Lord might send our way. At GGF the diversification of the church board came quite naturally. Deacon-trustees are nominated from the membership and approved by the elders before being ratified by the membership as a whole. It was several years into our experience as a multicultural church that I sat in a board meeting and looked around the table at the deacon-trustees who were deliberating on a particular issue. It occurred to me that among the nine deacons were three Caucasians, three Blacks and three Hispanics. This had occurred with no particular planning or forethought. It could certainly be attributed not only to the work of the Spirit among us, but also to an openness among members of the congregation to place qualified individuals, regardless of their ethnicity, in positions of leadership.

Shortly after this at a church business meeting some members of the congregation expressed their desire to see diversity on the pastoral staff. This request, which was taken seriously and prayerfully by church leaders, was met in a very clear and yet "natural" way by a qualified candidate (Shellie Sampson III). He was added, first to the congregation, and then recognized as an obvious choice for a position on the pastoral staff. The apparent lesson in our situation was that, although one must be willing to look beyond the customary places of finding ministry leaders, one must also have confidence that God will lead and provide qualified and gifted leaders for His people at the right time.

Another Methodist church in Texas, known as Church of the Disciple, was also begun with the intention of being culturally inclusive. Their music style reflected their commitment to diversity with a black keyboardist and a white soloist working together and using traditional hymns and black gospel music as well as Christian contemporary music to provide a balanced and varied menu. Although this church has struggled to find staff of color, it nonetheless demonstrates the importance of cultural diversity in its sermon themes. Front and center in the auditorium is a stained glass portrayal of the Last Supper where Jesus himself has darker skin tones and the rest of the disciples are pictured with multiple hues, suggesting people of varied colors representing the world's races and nationalities.[300]

Hawn describes another church that has transitioned from an historic Anglo church in the 1920's to one that is very diverse today but that has gone through many struggles in the shift. As the neighborhood surrounding the church changed, from being very affluent to one of apartment buildings and multifamily dwellings, the demographics also changed. In danger of closing in the 70's, Grace Methodist Church in Dallas saw a need to "reinvent itself." The church began programs to minister to the poor including a legal clinic and a medical clinic. This church struggled with leadership issues, the leadership being very white. It was "rare for a black person to achieve any management position."[301] Some members suggest that minorities added to committees are simply tokens.

Some Cambodians also attend the church but the language barrier continues to make it difficult to integrate them into the life of the church. Attention is given to ministry to the children of these Cambodian families. The motto adopted at Grace is "out of many, God makes us one" however there is criticism of separation and forced friendliness. Members express concern. One states, "I believe no matter how good our intentions are to be inclusive, many are simply uncomfortable with people who are, in many cases, so different from us." Others state, "we are glad they are here" but ask, "What happens when they outnumber us?"[302] Even the congregation that has decided to intentionally work toward developing diversity does not necessarily have an easy time of it.

It appears that the congregation that experiences the transition to a multicultural constituency has a number of greater challenges than those that are established with that stated goal in mind. Elizondo's question is crucial in determining readiness for diversity: "Does the congregation really want to be a multicultural family? . . . or . . . Does the congregation want continuity with just a bit more color and foreign accents?"[303] These descriptions of multicultural congregations give us the sense that man can try to do too much without a real sense of dependency on the work of the Spirit. "Except the Lord build the house, they labor in vain" (Ps. 127:1).

As previously mentioned, Yancey sees intentionality as one of the key elements in developing multicultural churches. He says:

> There is a powerful tendency among Christians to believe that if they just welcome people of other races then such individuals will eventually join their churches and an integrated congregation can develop. But multiracial churches do not just spring up. They are the result of intentional efforts on the part of church leaders and members to create or maintain an integrated congregation. . . . If the church does not put forth an intentional effort to help first-generation immigrants, then those immigrants are very unlikely to show up for worship. . . . the social trends of our society are so powerfully geared toward the maintenance of racial segregation that it is unreasonable to expect the development and the maintenance of multiracial congregations if the leaders of those congregations do not take intentional steps to make racial integration a reality.[304]

Raleigh Washington and Glen Kehrein argue that reconciliation will not occur unless Christians are willing to intentionally go out of their way to pursue relationships with people of other races.[305] This is critical. We can say that we are accepting of other peoples but unless we welcome them and invite them into our homes they will not feel "embraced." I believe this is critical as the testimony of the first African-American couple in our church illustrates. If it had not been for an invitation to dinner by an elder and his wife and the welcome they felt, they probably would not have stayed at Gracepoint. Indeed, if they had not stayed, having "broken the color barrier," it is questionable whether or not others would have come and stayed.

This suggests that church members cannot assume a laissez-faire attitude toward visitors of other races/ethnicities but must be willing to go out of their way to welcome and draw them into fellowship. Yancey says,

> The principle of intentionality conceptualizes the work necessary to overcome the inclination most of us have to stick to our own race. . . . intentionality is distinct from those other principles in that intentionality consists of the attitude that recognizes that achieving these other principles and developing a multiracial congregation will be the result of not accepting the normal way things are done in our society. This attitude enables us to be willing to go out of our way to become or maintain a multiracial congregation. . . . multiracial church growth is unlikely to happen by accident.[306]

It seems that there needs to be a balance in our approach here. Dependence on the Lord is absolutely necessary to see the miraculous occur. Diversity in a church in America is far from the norm. However, just to say "if it is the Lord's will it will happen," can be a rather indolent and slothful approach. At Gracepoint we prayed often for the Lord to bring people in from the North, South, East and West. There were Sunday mornings when the congregation turned to those four points of the compass and interceded for that harvest. We believe that what we now see on Sunday morning is an answer to those specific prayers.

There is no aspect of the Christian life that does not consist of a combination of human effort and divine working, or, should we say, our collaborating, working together, with the Spirit of the Lord. Paul and Apollos still had to plant and water although it was God who gave the growth. They were, as we are, "God's fellow workers" (1 Cor. 3:6,7). A diverse congregation is a "work of the Spirit" but it also a result of vision, of human effort, of a willingness to change what needs to be changed and a willingness to cooperate with the Spirit. He is the One who can place this desire within us. We are to partner with Him.

Spiritual growth is a work of the Spirit of God yet it requires commitment to spiritual disciplines. In the same way, the blessings of a multicultural congregation can only come through the Spirit's work in the hearts of men enabling them to see people with different eyes than before. He will enable us to transcend the differences of race and culture. However, we must be intentional in confronting sin in our life whether it is immorality, greed or prejudice. We must face selfishness and pride that may be demonstrated in our desire to worship our way or what we think is the right way. Intentionality may be seen as simply the willingness to see and think of the needs of others and let go of our "rights." "Each of you should look not to your own interests, but also to the interests of others" (Phil. 2:4, NIV).

Preparing the Local Church for Diversity

Yancey says that it is vital and necessary to prepare a congregation for changes that will come with the transition from a monoracial to a multiracial congregation. "It is foolish," he insists, "to believe that major changes are not going to occur in this transition. The members of the church must think about those changes and be ready to make the adjustments and sacrifices necessary for the transition to occur."[307] Programs that allow church members to interact with individuals of other races will better prepare the congregation. The church must be bringing people together in more than just a celebratory worship experience. Opportunities for fellowship and social interaction must be manifold meeting the needs of various kinds of people and their interests. Specific components of church life must be addressed in this preparation.

Prayer - At Gracepoint we have generally felt that diversity did indeed "just happen." In saying that, we recognize that there were factors that contributed to it and encouraged it. As previously mentioned, before the changes, we as a congregation would stop and <u>pray</u>, sometimes even on Sunday mornings, facing to the north, south, east and west, praying for God to bring in peoples from various towns within Rockland. This prepared our hearts for those He would send. Knowing that we were praying for the stranger to come in certainly made it easier to embrace them. The church was prepared through prayer and through Biblical teaching. The nature of our congregation was one that was very warm and welcoming, most of them going out of their way to acknowledge and greet the newcomer.

Preaching - Much of this preparation for diversity will come in sermons that lay out the values necessary for the task and the theological underpinnings of the message of reconciliation. Yancey suggests that there is one sin that the church seldom, if ever, preaches about – the sin of racism.[308] The white evangelical has often focused on the societal sin of abortion while ignoring the societal sins of racism and injustice. Meanwhile the black church has frequently and understandably done just the opposite.

"Sanctity of Human Life" Sunday, observed in many white congregations in remembrance of the infamous Roe v. Wade decision, has been seen as clashing with and overriding the significance of Martin Luther King Day by many blacks. It would seem that the logical solution to such a logjam is to give each its proper recognition and tie together the offenses of abortion and racism as contradictory of the Christian understanding of man made in the image of God and the value of every human life. Preaching the "whole counsel of God" is a necessary preparation for the changes that will inevitably come.

Worship style - Yancey makes the point that churches that are multiracial or moving in that direction are not free to limit their worship style to what one culture enjoys. They will incorporate different cultural styles into their worship. An important asset of diverse worship is that it lends itself to creating an attitude of racial acceptance. Yancey says:

> The challenge for multiracial churches is to find a balance of different worship styles that will enable these churches to attract members of different racial groups. . . . When a church limits its style of worship to only one racial culture it is sending out signals about who is supposed to be comfortable at its service. There is a subtle message that visitors to that church must either accept the racial environment of that church or find another place of worship.[309]

Inclusive worship music can be achieved by rotating the style each Sunday, by incorporating different styles each Sunday or by creating a completely new style through the writing of unique songs. Hawn states, "From the beginning of the Christian church, music and musicians have been a source of controversy."[310] Concern about pagan influences, conflict over types of musical instruments, the use of dance, and the styles of music – these are just some of the considerations in a multicultural worship setting. How can the music capture the vision of inclusiveness? Hawn suggests first of all, the congregation, rather than the choir, should be the primary choir of worship. The worship leader(s) must be one who communicates, "Sing with me" rather than "Listen to me."[311] He states:

> A good song, well taught and appropriately integrated into worship in itself unites those gathered as the body of Christ. . . . Music – sung, played or danced – has a capacity to weave itself into the fabric of an experience and to transform individuals into a vital singing, praying community. . . . What can be said, can be sung. Words spoken to the community may have power but words sung by all the people shape the community's identity.[312]

Places where Christianity is growing today most rapidly are "dancing cultures." Those from Euro-American cultures may resist dance and movement. They may feel self-conscious. Hawn seeks to encourage openness here,

> Many songs from the world church reflect cultures in which dance is a natural form of expression. . . . Many Westerners may have difficulty imagining cultures where singing and moving are integral experiences. For congregations striving to be more culturally conscious, moving and singing encourage hospitality and solidarity with those of other cultures who more naturally engage in this practice."[313]

The challenge is to provide a safe place for experimentation and also a comfort level when one does not participate.

This is a place to laugh and even to laugh at oneself. A choir or worship team may help to teach movement. Providing specific instructions will help at times. Certain songs will encourage movement. One should be free to sing or dance or to do both or to do nothing. The leader's role should be invitational, not coercive.[314]

One must also keep in mind that there is more to worship than music. Inclusive worship keeps in mind the décor of the building, the order of service, forms, ceremonies, liturgies, and even the length of the service. The data in the Lilly survey indicated that the average length of the predominantly white service was seventy minutes, the average time for predominantly black congregations was 105 minutes and the average multiracial service was something of a compromise at eighty-three minutes.[315] It would be helpful to know the differences within various denominations as well in order to do appropriate comparisons.

Diverse leadership - Another item of tremendous significance in preparing for a mixed attendance is the matter of diverse leadership. The Jerusalem church modeled this. In the midst of its first conflict involving Aramaic and Greek speaking Jews, the apostles seemed to recognize the value of inclusive leadership. They showed wisdom in laying hands on servant leaders, chosen by the people. It is certainly no coincidence that they had Greek names (Acts 6:1-6). Kenneth

Barker comments, "The murmuring had come from the Greek-speaking segment of the church; so those elected to care for the work came from their number so as to represent their interests fairly."[316] African-Americans have expressed the need for their children to see black men as godly role models because those role models have historically been lacking. An integrated leadership will attract people of different ethnicities and color.

How does one achieve a leadership that is ethnically mixed without quotas and without preferential treatment in preparing and selecting leaders? God can and will supply leaders of various ethnic backgrounds in answer to prayer.[317] In the early church, leaders were called by the Spirit in answer to prayer and set apart for ministry in the midst of prayer and fasting (Acts 13:2). Yancey again comments:

> In a multiracial church people are often concerned that their racial group will be ignored when it comes to decision-making. . . . Multiracial leadership increases the chance that the decision makers of the church will be sensitive to the perspectives of people of different races. This type of leadership models racial acceptance for the members of that church and creates an atmosphere of racial tolerance.[318]

Leadership is also tied to intentionality because we tend to have friends and contacts within our own race and thus tend to find leaders who are like ourselves.[319] We often have a bias that induces us to choose a person similar to us. Yancey says, "When we do not recognize the power of our cultural biases, we often fail to see how we justify the leadership potential of a prospective leader upon our own cultural bias instead of upon a scripturally based criteria."[320] The challenge is to find leaders who are in agreement in theological matters, who share a similar philosophy of ministry and who have the ministry skills that are necessary. It takes extra effort to find leaders of different races. One must be proactive. Yancey notes that African-Americans face a greater degree of alienation in society and thus they need more assurance than other racial groups that their concerns will be heard. It certainly makes sense that if any one particular racial or ethnic group is being targeted, that a member of that group should be included in the leadership structure of the church.

Overarching goal - Diverse leadership will promote inclusive worship. It will also affect the overarching goal of the church. Yancey suggests, "Church leaders who want to create a multiracial ministry are wise not to put the main focus of their church on the effort to be a multiracial congregation. . . . efforts to become multiracial should be in the context of the larger goals of a church."[321] Overarching goals may be evangelism for the evangelical church, serving the neighborhood for the Roman Catholic parish, and dealing with structural sins and social justice for the mainline denominational church. Yancey concludes, "Sometimes a direct approach is not the best answer to a problem. A church leader can sometimes alienate church members through an overt multiracial emphasis. If church leaders desire to minimize resistance from church attendees, it is valuable for a multiracial emphasis to be tied to nonracial overarching goals."[322] Once these goals are established it may be seen, or the case be made by leaders, that becoming multiracial is important to achieving the goal.

Location - The matters of location, personal skills, and adaptability can all be tied to intentionality. "White flight" has been a pattern for individuals and for churches for decades. "People of color understand that whites are less willing to live in integrated neighborhoods than they are. This understanding helps explain why white flight is insulting to people of color."[323] A church may decide, rather than following members of the congregation to the suburbs, to intentionally stay in an urban area in order to minister to those moving into the neighborhood. Some churches are actually deciding to move to an urban area or a more diverse community to reach out to that diverse population and thus to attain the goal of multi-ethnicity. Other churches, in the suburbs or rural communities are finding, due to changing demographics, great opportunities to reach out to minorities. Individual Christians are determining to stay in a changing neighborhood or to intentionally move into an urban and diverse community in response to what they sense is the will and call of God for them.

Personal skills - If a multicultural congregation is desired, certain personal skills need to be developed, particularly by church leaders. These include the following qualities: sensitivity to different needs, patience, ability to empower other individuals and the capacity to relate to those of different races. Although the pastor of the monoracial congregation has need of these qualities, the pastor of the multiracial church may need "a double portion." According to Yancey the sensitivity required of the leader has two dimensions. The first "involves the ability to receive, evaluate and appropriately handle criticism that may come because of the church's attempt to create a multiracial atmosphere."[324] The pastor may be required to deal with unfair criticism and thus need to develop 'a thick skin.' He needs to listen to the message behind what is being said rather than react defensively.

The second dimension of this sensitivity consists of the ability to adjust to various cultures and to overcome cultural ignorance. One must be willing to listen to others and learn from his mistakes; to apologize when appropriate, rather than trying to justify an improper response. I have had to change my speech more than once to ensure that I am not offending a group by my words or expressions. What we think is humorous can be insulting or degrading to others. Using bad grammar to caricature the African-American is an example. "Generally, European Americans are more ignorant about the cultures of racial minorities than vice versa."[325]

A pastor or church leader must display patience in order to overcome and to address the dysfunctional race relations of the past four hundred years, the lack of trust that has accumulated, the residual racism that remains, and the many misunderstandings and offenses that result from a lack of knowledge of and sensitivity to another's culture. Spencer Perkins and Chris Rice make a case that meetings where blacks and whites discuss their true feelings about race are necessary because "relationships between blacks and whites in America have been so strained that the trust needed to begin and sustain a relationship does not always come easily."[326] The pastor must empower others, particularly those who are not members of the numerical majority, to deal with issues that arise lest he be like Moses, trying to carry the weight of the multitude on his own shoulders. Finally, this leader must become skilled at relating to those of different races and cultures. In order to relate effectively it will take a great deal of listening, learning, and openness to change.

Adaptability - According to the research done by Yancey, the last characteristic of the church that attracts other ethnicities is "adaptability." "We must," Perkins and Rice write, "anticipate the changes a multicultural congregation will bring and, if possible, prepare for them. . . . we must be ready to adapt and change previous ideas and practices that may work in a monoracial setting but not in a multiracial one."[327] Current church members must be willing to make changes to accommodate newcomers rather than expecting them to simply conform to existing church practices. A church may need to accommodate immigrants with live translation or with headsets that will allow them to hear what is being said in their own tongue. Signs written in the language of another people group, and décor to which they might relate, conveys a sense of respect for other cultures. Acceptance of biracial marriages and multiracial families is crucial. Cultural norms of the numerical majority cannot be so inflexible that people who were not socialized in that racial culture will be constantly uncomfortable. Ethnocentrism must be surrendered. Once again, leadership will be key to the ability of any congregation to adjust and adapt.

Churches, according to Hawn, can be classified according to four different approaches as relates to cultural sensitivity. Understanding where one's church falls on this spectrum allows leadership to evaluate how prepared the congregation is for diversity. The first of the four approaches defines worship from one particular cultural perspective. This is labeled cultural uniformity, where those who gather for worship are on the same cultural page, with common backgrounds and a similar way of viewing the world.[328] This uniformity is often found in a minority context where worship helps to maintain a cultural heritage.[329] African-Americans and Asians, for example, often sense a need to preserve cultural values and identity and their style of worship reinforces these passions. (It should not be assumed that faithful and vital worship cannot take place in congregations that are culturally homogeneous.)

The truth is however, that cultural uniformity is becoming more and more difficult to achieve, or to hold onto, than ever before. Patterns of migration, global communication and marriage across ethnic and racial lines make it almost impossible to have cultural uniformity yet, amazingly, many churches still do. Generational differences have some of the same effects as varied ethnic perspectives within a congregation. In many churches today the minister addresses four very distinct generations (builders, boomers, busters and gen-xer's) with widely different worldviews and experiences. Children of immigrants quickly embrace a new culture and values that are foreign to their parents. Hawn believes that culturally uniform worship does not prepare the body of Christ to engage with a diverse and complex society.[330] It runs the risk of excluding those who are different while cutting individuals off from those who might enrich them. Thornburg states, "Cliques provide security, but not transformation" and Hawn concludes, "True worship should enable worshipers to become transformed from being separate cliques to being the body of Christ."[331]

Cultural assimilation is the second approach. "This practice assumes a dominant cultural perspective that will become the common currency for all."[332] Some worshipers are seeking this goal because they have come to accept and prefer the cultural ethos of the dominant group. If one joins the Eastern Orthodox Church, for example, one is being linked to a liturgy and practice that has basically stayed the same since 1054 A.D., with little or no cultural change. Likewise, one might affiliate with an African-American church specifically because he enjoys and appreciates the style of music and preaching found there. Some African-Americans chose a white church in the 1960's and 70's simply to claim their right to integration. In those years, integration in church meant assimilation to the dominant culture. Even now immigrant groups may chose a white church to practice their English and learn cultural norms of their new country. They are attempting to "fit in," assuming that they have little or no power to change that environment.[333]

These churches may invite minorities from the community to worship with them but those invited will inevitably sense a "disconnect" between the words, "All are welcome here" and the nonverbal communication they experience. Nonverbal signs include such things as a lack of minorities in leadership, a non-inclusive worship style, and artwork reflecting only the tastes of the majority. Worship, décor or non-inclusive leadership announces to them, "We are glad to do things for you, but you are really not one of us."[334]

The third position is titled cultural openness. Churches within this group display a spirit of receptivity toward the community's cultural diversity, even though the congregation may have a distinct cultural majority group. These churches include people from minority groups in decision-making roles and honor the cultural heritage of newcomers in the worship life of their churches. The majority group allows its worldview to be altered by the minority constituency in their decision-making processes and in their worship.[335]

Lastly, a congregation may reflect what is labeled cultural partnership. In this model there is no majority that dominates. Diverse members reflect the community and work together in shared Christian community.[336] There are no strangers and aliens, but all are fellow citizens. The vision of Ephesians 2 is a reality. Christ creates a mosaic that allows for rich possibilities for worship. Cultural partnership encourages worship that more fully embodies the diversity of God's creation as reflected in the humanity around us.

It would be beneficial for any congregation to evaluate where they are on the spectrum and the things that must be addressed if they desire to be a "culturally conscious" congregation. Hawn also points out, in his analysis of the "Nairobi Statement on Worship and Culture," that worship is transcultural, contextual, countercultural, and cross-cultural.[337] A multicultural congregation or one that is attempting to move in that direction should be cognizant of these concepts. The trans-cultural points to elements of worship that all Christians share in common such as Scripture reading and exposition, prayer, creeds, the recitation of the Lord's Prayer, baptism in water, and a sense of mission.[338] Incorporating these elements allows one to discern the common ground existent among very diverse groups and congregations.

Contextual worship pertains to things that are unique or uniquely expressed in local congregations. For example:

> How does the congregation gather?
> With silence or with conversation?
> With food or with singing?
> How is the Word read and proclaimed?
> How many lessons or scriptures are read?
> Who reads them?
> Are they sung or dramatized?
> How long is the sermon?
> From where is it delivered?
> How do the congregants respond (verbally, physically, silently)?
> What is the focus of the sermon (narratives, didactic, exposition, or application)?

The list of these kinds of questions is endless. Some matters are determined by denominational practice. Others are definitely cultural. Customs that intentionally exclude or devalue the practices of other believers can be a sign of prejudice and ethnocentrism. Understanding the relationship between the trans-cultural and the contextual will help to prevent the elevation of the contextual to the status of that which is trans-cultural, and help to avoid the forcing of others to conform to what are non-essentials.

The countercultural is the element of worship that runs contrary to the culture of the world. Hawn states, "All cultures have practices that are hostile to God's desires for humanity."[339] He continues, "In an attempt to employ meaningful elements from various cultural settings in culturally conscious worship, one must discern what aspects of culture strengthen the gathered body of Christ and what elements may be contrary to God's created order." An illustration of this would be "rituals that render some voiceless or invisible by denying their worth as children of God."[340] Worship practices may encourage segregation and promote classism when they reserve fixed roles for a certain ages, genders, races, or social classes.[341] The distinctive roles of clergy and laity need to be considered here.

The last section of the *Nairobi Statement* speaks of worship as cross-cultural. Because he is the Savior of all people, the statement says, Christ "welcomes the treasures of the earthly cultures into the city of God . . ." namely, "music, art, architecture, gestures and postures, and other elements of different cultures."[342] It is for each church to determine exactly how to achieve a cross-cultural style of worship appropriate to their setting. Many Native Americans who became Christians had to relinquish key elements of their culture. Their drums were, at one time, labeled as of the devil. Their long hair was cut. Today there is, thankfully, some affirmation of aspects of culture that were formerly denounced as less than Christian or even demonic.

Hawn's list of stylistic aspects of a congregation's "corporate inner life" prompts one to consider the many details that might attract or repel people of a different culture:

> How are people greeted?
> Does the officiate wear vestments?
> How do the choir and other worship leaders enter the worship space?
> What is the music that is sung? Is it fast or slow, loud or soft? What is the style?
> What instruments accompany the music?
> Do people move and sway or stand still when they sing?
> How are visitors (strangers) made welcome?
> What is the role of silence in worship?
> What is the shape of the worship space?
> What symbols are displayed?
> How is the communion table prepared?
> How do people receive communion?
> How is the Scripture introduced?
> What does this congregation call the worship space – sanctuary, auditorium, nave, or chancel?
> Is a printed order of worship used?[343]

All of these items constitute the nonverbal ethos of worship. They "form a matrix of impressions reflecting the style and the inner piety of a congregation."[344] Hawn asks, "How can we avoid a knee-jerk reaction when we encounter the worship of others? How can we avoid judging too quickly with 'I like it' or 'I don't'?"[345] Lane declares, "We have a choice. We can respond with either: xenophobia – the fear of other cultures; ethnocentrism – believing one's culture is superior; segregationist – wanting cultures to coexist separately; accepting – wanting others to become like us; or celebrating – learning from and enjoying the diversity of others."[346] Obviously, the last response is most desirable in building multicultural congregations.

Understanding Other Cultures

"Racism is real," says Lane, "and it is destructive and wrong, but one place to begin to eliminate it is to begin to understand cultural differences."[347] Lane states that immigrants quickly adapt to the dominant culture in externals (clothing, greetings, diet, and language). These things are the easiest and most likely to change. However, below the surface, is the internal part of culture that motivates external behavior. It consists of beliefs and worldview. The age of an individual, the community he lives in, the faith he embraces, and one's knowledge and employment of the majority language, are all factors that determine how quickly and how deeply one adapts to another culture.[348] It is helpful to realize that people who come into one's church may appear outwardly to be "American" while still retaining the values and beliefs of their nation of origin.

Lane quotes Robert Hughes, "The future of America 'in a globalized economy without a cold war will rest with people who can think and act with informed grace across ethnic, cultural, and linguistic lines. And the first step lies in acknowledging that we are not one big world family, or ever likely to be . . . in the world that is coming, if you can't navigate differences, you've had it.' "[349] She then analyzes six different aspects of culture that those who are interacting with peoples of differing cultures need to be attuned to.

First, there are high and low context cultures. High context cultures place a great amount of meaning on the "context" including: environment, process, body language, and appearance. For this person experience is equal to fact, the context of an event is as important as the event itself, there is no distinction between the idea and the person, the group is important, relationships are of utmost importance and life is viewed holistically.[350] Low context cultures focus on individuality and value efficiency. Second, a distinction is made between being and doing cultures. Being cultures value relationships and the quality of life. Doing cultures value results and materialism. In being cultures results are seen from the perspective of relationship, and in doing cultures relationships are seen from the perspective of accomplishment.[351] These approaches certainly affect our values and our priorities. One might ask if one approach is more Biblical than the other and the answer might reveal that the majority culture in America is "less Biblical."

Third, there is the <u>influence and perception of authority</u>. Egalitarian cultures believe that all persons have equal value and equal rights. "In hierarchal cultures the unequal treatment of persons is not only accepted but also considered appropriate."[352] These cultures value people according to gender, race, caste, and so on. Leadership and status are viewed very differently by dissimilar cultures. Anthropologist Geert Hofstede gives insight into the issue of high distance and low distance cultures. People who come from high-power-distance cultures see themselves as relatively powerless before an elite group who hold the wealth and make decisions. This elite group rules at the top of a pyramid while the vast majority, making up the base of the pyramid, have little opportunity to make significant changes due to a lack of education and economic means.

In low-power-distance cultures, on the other hand, many more people, a large middle class, feel they have a say and have the possibility to make changes since they have educational and economic opportunities. This can be an important factor in multicultural congregations.[353] Without an understanding of this dynamic, congregants will fail to comprehend why some will not respond to the invitation to join in decision-making processes and how to involve them. One's view of authority may make it unlikely that a person would question or debate an issue with that authority. Foster says, "Diverse ethnic groups bring with them culturally conditioned understandings of those in authority and leadership."[354]

Fourth, there are <u>collective and individual cultures</u>. Collective cultures view themselves as part of a group. Individualistic cultures see each person as an individual, separate from family or community. Low context cultures tend to be individualistic.[355] In collective cultures there is a great fear of "losing face" which brings shame to a person and to his family or people. Many actions may be taken to ensure that one does not lose face (i.e. being complementary, not asking questions that will force the person to admit a mistake, showing respect). Americans, as part of an individualistic culture, value self-reliance, autonomy, and personal rights and fear the loss of autonomy that would be characteristic of a collective culture.[356]

We should also be aware of the <u>diverse views of time</u> in different cultures. Lane notes, "Usually the first cultural difference I hear people talk about is the difference in dealing with time."[357] One culture starts on time according to the clock. These "clock-watchers" are too rigid for others who start when all the people who need to be there are there. That is indicative of a "being culture." Services may be long or short depending on one's cultural framework. An Anglo Presbyterian service may be sixty minutes or less. A Hispanic Pentecostal service may last for three hours. In fact some groups will not feel that they have had 'church' unless it lasts for at least two hours. Some want to 'get to the point' and cut back on any excess preliminaries or extraneous announcements. Others are in no hurry to get on with the service. Expectations will certainly affect one's degree of satisfaction with the worship experience. Understanding other cultures' "clocks" will promote better relationships.[358]

Anthropologist Edward Hall distinguishes between 'monochronic' and 'polychronic' senses of time. The monochronic view of time is most often associated with Euro-Americans who believe that time is saved or wasted, lost or made up. They are concerned about being late or being too early, about taking too much time. They sing hymns that are sequential, one stanza leading into the next with a sense of direction and purpose. Other peoples have a polychronic sense of time. Time is less sequential and more relational. Being with others is never a waste of time. In fact, in Tanzania, the expression used when waiting for others to start the church service is "making time" not "wasting time." Time is more cyclical than linear. These groups are able to savor the moment and put other things on hold. Their songs tend to be repetitive and open-ended. They generally involve a physical response and thus include a visible expression with the music. Hymnals are seldom used and the words and music are heard and internalized more quickly.[359]

The last area to consider is the difference in worldviews that are often a factor of culture. Worldviews are categorized as "pre-modern," modern and "post-modern." Animism would be an example of a pre-modern view. Pre-modern and post-modern thinkers accept spiritual realities more easily than do modern thinkers. Pre-modern thinkers accept what are seen as inconsistencies and incongruities to others. Postmodern and modern thinkers need verification but accept it in different forms – the modern thinker through scientific study and the postmodern through experience.

Lane states, "Different worldviews can be a barrier to good communication and relationships at a deeper level."[360] She goes on to add, "The power of worldview is enormous because it sets the boundaries for what one understands as reality" and cautions that "Much of what is called Christian in the United States is really syncretism, a blending of U. S. cultural values and Christian teaching into a system that reflects more of who we are culturally than who God has called us to be as his followers."[361] Converts are often requested to adopt cultural values rather than Biblical values. There is no room given for the Holy Spirit to reveal how God would have one's faith expressed through that particular culture. We may imply that people must leave their culture behind and adopt that of the messenger.[362]

Hofstede also studied cultural characteristics adding such ideas as immediacy, masculinity and uncertainty. High contact cultures are characterized by immediacy - eye contact, smiling, standing in close proximity, and touching. Masculinity points to strength, assertiveness and competitiveness versus attributes of femininity - affection, compassion and nurturance. Uncertainty refers to the culture's ability to tolerate risk, uncertainty, and ambiguity.

We must understand the inevitably of conflict as a result of cultural differences. "No matter how carefully you examine each cultural lens, a disagreement, conflict or miscommunication will occur." In fact, Lane suggests, "In a cross-cultural relationship often at least some aspect of the problem is culturally based."[363] She summarizes, "By understanding these six lenses and their impact on who we are and who others are, we will be better able to establish relationships with people from other cultures. . . . Once we recognize our own perspective we can begin to look at those around us and accept the perspective from which they see the world."[364] Our culture often influences what we believe is "Christian." Examining the cultures of others allows us to test these presuppositions.

Another concern is that of nonverbal clues. Euro-Americans pay more attention to what is said or written. Many other cultures see the spoken or written word verified in what is done or displayed. If a welcome statement is printed but not supported by nonverbal actions, it is meaningless. If Christ is portrayed as white and if other symbols lack meaning to people of color, if there is little time to greet one another, what is seen and felt may contradict what is written or spoken.[365] It will be helpful for those of a majority culture in a church to visit a church where they are part of the minority in order to better understand the conditions that make one feel welcome or unwelcome.

Also, there is the matter of a detailed, written order of service versus an order of service that is very brief or non-existent. If a church has an "oral tradition" it is likely to sing more, to be more intergenerational and more interactive – to take 'detours' which often build community and to make room for children.[366] Hawn says, "the relative balance of oral versus written tradition in worship may be a challenge for culturally conscious congregations as they learn to worship together. Avoiding this issue, however, may hamper full participation by people of diverse cultures."[367]

(4) The Vision to Be Embraced
What is the ideal?

Peart has developed another way of categorizing churches. According to him, churches today fall into one of five categories or models of reconciliation: segregation, differentiation, assimilation, intentional, but irrational, and lastly, what he calls, "inHIMtegration."[368] The segregated congregation obviously will not attract, but instead repel visitors of another race or ethnicity. An extreme example of this type of church was Temple Baptist Church, numbering 5,000 in attendance, but having an unwritten policy of not allowing African-Americans into their membership. This policy was not changed until 1986. Such a church believes that the separation of the races is God-ordained and that one race is superior to another. This type of church operates with the premise that people of another color would be better off in a church with people of the same race. There is a fear that integration will result in interracial marriages which are regularly condemned using "Biblical" support. President Carter was a member of a church in Plains, Georgia that barred blacks from services until a vote of the membership finally rescinded that policy in 1976.

The differentiation church is also exclusive in that it chooses not to attract individuals of another race. The leadership believes that accepting individuals of different culture will force church members to "give up the expression of their racial and cultural uniqueness in their church gatherings."[369] Often this uniqueness is the language spoken by members but it may also be seen in distinctives such as dress, food, or music. Among ethnic groups there is often great resistance to worshiping in another language and a fear of losing one's heritage and uniqueness. This type of church has its place in that it reaches a specific population where individuals are not yet fluent in English. However, even a church of this persuasion must be challenged not to be so proud of its heritage that people of other ethnic groups are not welcomed when they enter.

Churches that are inclusive in composition are categorized under Peart's "assimilation" model. In these types of churches people of a different race or ethnicity are welcomed but only if they adjust in order to 'fit in.' If they continue to retain their distinctiveness, they will eventually become a church within the church. This is because there is no attempt, on the part of the majority population, to change to accommodate the newcomers. Music styles and curriculum remain exactly the same no matter who is being ministered to. Missionary church plants in various countries have often required those of other cultures to conform to the culture of the dominant or planting group. This attitude that one must become like us to worship with us can be seen not only in white churches, but in ethnic churches as well.

The mind-set stems from a fear that diversity will "rock the boat" or "upset the apple cart." There is a "unity" and a comfort in similarity that avoids the challenge of diversity. Differences are only emphasized as a part of a special program or presentation. Leaders may believe that reconciliation has taken place when the minority conforms and submits to the majority.[370] A church may open its doors to another congregation to share its facility and, at times, to participate in combined services. Of course this seldom means that ownership or power is shared.

The assimilation model is the easiest and the safest of the inclusive models. The burden for change is on the minority group. "This model is familiar to most Christians since it mirrors the system of integration that is operating in the world."[371] Integration is the human attempt to accomplish a reconciliation that is really possible only with divine aid. Peart says, "When mere integration is the focus, the effort is to move diverse racial groups into close social, economic and political relationships to obtain for minority groups political power and equality. Therefore, representation is the measure of success rather than reconciliation."[372] Martin Luther King described a move to end segregation in these terms: "It leaves us with a stagnant sense of sameness rather than a constructive equality of oneness."[373] Contrasted with this, true Biblical reconciliation brings a change in one's heart toward others.

There is recognition of equality in Christ and a new approach to "power." The quest for equal power will not solve the problem of racism. The Scripture demands mutual submission within the household of faith (Eph. 5:21). It is only as the concern for "power" is set aside and there is a willingness to serve others that there can be true reconciliation.

Another inclusive approach is labeled "<u>intentional but irrational</u>." This is a ministry that works to bring in other ethnicities and allows these ethnicities to express themselves throughout the ministry. There is a sincere attempt to prevent the racial and ethnic issues of society from affecting the unity of the group. However, Peart points out that there is a fatal flaw in this approach: "there is a written or unwritten policy to not differentiate on the basis of race. This approach creates an irrational or artificial environment that only exists when and where the church's members gather. Under this policy, the church does not transform the prejudices and thoughts of its members by addressing them openly through truth and love, but rather attempts to suppress them for the sake of unity."[374]

Peart uses Circle Church as an illustration of this particular church model - a multicultural, multiracial church in Chicago that sought to manifest Biblical reconciliation. However, the unwillingness or reticence to address race issues from black and white perspectives, led to the dominance of one view over another. The church eventually split along racial lines. If unity means that no one can voice discontent or displeasure, then no racial issues will be expressed because the issues are thought to be contentious. Racism is not dealt with. It is assumed that problems in the world are of no concern to the church. Peart objects, "The leader erroneously views the church as other-worldly in mission rather than "counter-world."[375] The present world system is seen as irrelevant. A counter-world community demands that the erroneous views of the present world system be openly addressed and argued against. Adherents of a counter world community intentionally seek to live defying the false system within which they operate.

Reconciliation does not mean that we deny or negate our differences. Men are still men and women are women, in the Body of Christ. We are still what we always were, however, these differences do not prevent us from fellowshipping together. "True fellowship based on reconciliation is fellowship that goes beyond our similarities and glories in the fact that, although we have differences, yet we are one. The inability of the intentional but irrational church type hinders its ability to reconcile its members and to impact the world system."[376] Glen Stassen says,

> Justice rather than reconciliation is the better rubric under which to consider issues of race. More precisely,

we want to argue that both biblically and in the context of historic patterns of racial injustice in the United States, the concept of reconciliation is empty of content unless it is built upon the sturdy foundation of justice. If reconciliation is understood as the repair of broken relationships and the restoration of trusting and intimate community between persons or groups, then justice is its first step. There can be no racial reconciliation unless there is first the redress of race-based or race-linked injustice, just as there can generally be no reconciliation between alienated persons or groups until or unless previous and current wrongs are constructively addressed. While the language of racial reconciliation continues to carry the day in most Christian circles, seemingly unquestioned, it is precisely over issues of racial justice that white and black Americans tend to disagree most vigorously.[377]

The last category of church into which Peart groups churches is what he labels, "inHIMtegration," a term he coined to describe the new humanity of Ephesians 2:

When a church makes intentional choices to mix, accept, represent and manifest racial and ethnic differences, but at the same time magnifies to a greater extent the oneness of believers in Christ, I call it inHIMtegration. . . This new creation now neutralizes all worldly divisions and becomes the epitome of integration for all those who are in him. In this model intentional efforts are made to address issues and differences so that they can then be dealt with in healthy ways. Then and only then can the Holy Spirit be free to heal and unify believers into the reality of their oneness.[378]

Diversity training or integration fails as it mixes the races and hopes for changes in attitudes. *InHimtegration* starts with a premise: "that all are one in Christ and must not live the divisiveness that surrounds them." We are to "challenge the erroneous beliefs and actions we see around us."[379] "Be transformed," the apostle says, "by the renewing of your mind" (Rom. 12:1). You change hearts by changing heads.

Peart commends the Promise Keeper movement for illustrating how to accomplish this renewal. Bringing races and cultures together is a priority in their gatherings. The word of God is used to speak directly to the issue of racism. The subjects of ownership of and forgiveness for discrimination have been addressed. Attendees are challenged to live out their oneness in Christ. There is recognition of racism in every aspect of society yet at the same time there is a focus on the unity of believers in Christ. Individuals are able to take pride in one's culture as an aspect of his/her identity in Christ.

The Jerusalem council in Acts 15 is an illustration of this model. Gentiles had come to faith through the preaching of Paul and Barnabus. Men from Judea challenged their conversion insisting that these Gentiles must first become Jews, conforming to practices of the law before they could be saved. Paul and Barnabus were sent to Jerusalem to help sort out these divisive issues with the apostles. Although the leadership of the church was almost exclusively Jewish, the group rejected the need for Gentiles to become Jews before being added to the church. These Gentiles were actually encouraged to hold onto their cultural distinctiveness while adhering to certain essentials of the faith (Acts 15:10f, 28f). These essentials allowed for peaceful coexistence and the mutual edification of Jewish and Gentile believers.

The actions of this council are set forth as an ideal model of Biblical reconciliation. Reconciliation may be seen in the presence of diverse races and cultural expressions, heard in the style of music and preaching, and felt in the fellowship of believers through tangible actions and expressed concerns. We can achieve this model in various ways. A homogeneous church may reach out to, and welcome other ethnic groups, by simply welcoming "people." A church may be planted with the specific intention to be a multicultural congregation. Two or three churches ministering to various ethnic groups may decide to merge. A church may develop ministries to different ethnic groups within the same facility, with the same church name but different worship services, Bible studies and fellowship times. Any of these may be legitimate approaches to inHIMtegration.

How Do We Get There?

The goal of a multicultural congregation is a seldom realized but nevertheless worthy goal to strive for. Ireland suggests, "Although a three-percentile figure is extremely low, the mere existence of the multiracial church may prove that implementable principles to combat 'the most segregated hour' in America . . . exist."[380] How will the number of these churches multiply during the next generation? According to Foster, "Congregations discover new possibilities for their future through their responsiveness to people who do not share their racial and/or cultural heritage."[381] Eugene says:

> The vocabulary of multiculturalism has helped the church see the complexities of the issue without necessarily providing a great deal of guidance about what to do. That cultures in their integrity should be esteemed and affirmed; that cultural differences should be celebrated, not repressed; that it is not simply a matter of accommodating minority cultures to the dominant culture, but also the other way around – all of this is accepted by most people trying to be sensitive to the human and pastoral needs of diverse groups. Likewise, conservative critics have made us aware that the language of multiculturalism can be misused. It has been wielded as a weapon to bash western European cultures, and to promote often uncritical agendas of self-interest (e.g. Bloom 1988; D'Souza 1991).[382]

Wilson writes,

> For many reasons Christian communities often became single language and/or ethnic populations. However, such singular cultural fellowships were not meant to be the norm but only a transitory entity. When occasions made it possible, they were expected to reclaim

their true identity as a Pentecost fellowship, embracing the fullest possible plurality of the community in a given context.[383]

Black lists nine motivations for minorities to join themselves to a congregation of another ethnicity. The first two, "integration and assimilation," entail the willingness to give up one's own culture or style of worship for some benefit, social or economic, that is envisioned in joining and conforming to the majority in a given congregation. The third, "denominational loyalty," is decreasing in the U. S., although many immigrants still feel that attraction to the familiarity of their own denomination. Some may attend a church of another ethnicity because it shares a "common language" while others simply go to the closest parish (particularly Roman Catholics). There are those who are looking for "acceptance" who have not found it in a church of their own culture. One may be drawn to a multicultural church because of the needs that exist there and the sense that one can "make a difference." Many choose a multicultural church because it matches their experience in other areas of their life (school, work, recreation, etc.). A multicultural church is the obvious choice for those who have a "mixed marriage" and a multicultural family. Black concludes her list of motivations with "justice-oriented" and summarizes the desire and intent of many moving in this direction:

There are people from a wide variety of cultures who are convinced that the biblical mandate to strive for justice and peace on earth requires people to cross boundaries, to negotiate differences, and to work toward a sense of well-being for all. . . . They want to be changed by interchange, to be reformed by new insights, to be inspired by new rhythms and songs. As our society becomes more multicultural, there is a sense of urgency. If we cannot learn how to be truly multicultural in the church - each shaping the other and creating a common culture from the mix - we cannot expect peace across ethnicities and justice across cultures for our society, let alone the world. Persons join congregations expecting that their presence will make a difference, that their cultural affinities will challenge some of the status quo, that their racial heritage will affect some of the power dynamics in the church, and that their . . . expressions of spirituality will influence the form and content of worship.[384]

Foster sees the catalysts to "practices that embrace" as fourfold. The first of these, he says, is simply the "quest for survival." A congregation may rent to an ethnic group simply because it needs help paying expenses. This arrangement may lead to cooperation in an area like Christian education of children or evangelism. Cooperation and unity can develop. The second is labeled "gospel commitment" where a church intentionally decides to reach out to those who are not like themselves. There is an acknowledgement of the mission field at one's doorstep, that it includes those not like us.

The third catalyst is hospitality to the racial, cultural diversity that they find in their neighborhood. We must truly welcome any and all. Conde-Frazier says, "The first step in multicultural living is hospitality. It is a practice that brings us into closer alignment with the basic values of the kingdom. It is part of worshiping Jesus."[385] This includes making strangers feel welcome. "Hospitable congregations typically do not expect to be changed by those they welcome into their lives. And yet, as the biblical witness repeatedly indicates, strangers do impact the experience of those they meet."[386] The fourth catalyst that Foster notes is that of <u>theological vision</u>. Leaders envision a new kind of congregation or community. "The theological vision of many culturally and racially diverse congregations has been developed into mission statements and summarized in their publicity" using church names and expressions such as "The Church Where the World Worships, Church of All Nations," or "A Welcoming Community."[387]

Only one article related to the multicultural church was found in the Christian periodical "Leadership" at the time this research was done. The church described in this article was not really a "multicultural congregation" but it had embraced a "multicongregational plan." It was a church that illustrated the "quest for survival." The church opened its doors to various ethnic churches and allowed them to rent their facilities. Each of the ethnic churches was an autonomous congregation and had its own plan and mission. The congregations did not worship together or interact except in passing. They were linked only "through the denominational organization, an intercongregational steering committee and the commitment of the pastoral team to one another's ministry."[388] The benefits, however, of this arrangement were twofold: people with a heart for ministry in a cross-cultural setting were attracted to the Anglo congregation; the second generation of the ethnic churches were generally attracted to the English-speaking services, thus helping the Anglo congregation to realize the goal of becoming multicultural. A legitimate aim of a white or majority congregation is to attract the second generation of the ethnic church since the ethnic church generally loses a huge majority of its young people. It is estimated that Korean churches in New York City, for example, are losing approximately 90% of their younger generation, according to Dr. Mackenzie Pier, President of the NYC Leadership Center. In order to see these youth remain in or return to the Church it will be necessary for multicultural churches to open their doors to and attract these ethnic young people. A significant part of the growth of Redeemer Presbyterian Church in NYC may be attributed to this kind of ministry.

Even the initially segregated arrangement resulted in the need to understand one another's cultures in order to get along and to solve rather than spiritualize problems.[389] The host congregation began to give themselves "consciously to the people of other cultures" expressing concern and support for immigrants – helping them acquire a driver's license, negotiating visa troubles, assisting them in opening a bank account, or in finding employment. They began to realize the desperate needs of foreigners and the ways they could "practice Christian hospitality toward these people by giving little more than a caring heart and an investment of time."[390] Assistance was given while respecting the autonomy of their congregation and thus avoiding paternalism. There are groups that retain a vital need to worship in their own language and to hold on to their culture. The "quest for survival" had moved the host church toward "gospel commitment."

The third catalyst, hospitality, is repeatedly seen as all-important. Lloyd states, "we aim to be hospitable, to make the stranger feel welcome. It's amazing how quickly a smile and a helping hand bridge even the highest of cultural barriers."[391] Foster relates, "The pastor of one congregation instructs the congregation after the benediction to give each other 'a handshake, a hug, or a kiss' legitimating in the process several cultural approaches to greeting each other."[392] However, there must be more than an appropriate welcome to develop a multicultural body of believers that truly reflects what the church is intended to be. There must be continuing contact and cooperation in ministry that allows for the development of cross-cultural relationships and friendships. Ireland encourages analyzing the ways these relationships are formed and sustained.[393]

The fourth catalyst, that of theological vision, leads to another item of concern for establishing a culturally conscious worship - the matter of leadership. Leadership is key. "The leaders in any organization must be the environmental change agents," says John Maxwell.[394] Without godly and dedicated leaders the ideal of biblical reconciliation will not be achieved. There will be no expressed vision to pursue it. Ireland summarizes the results of research, "Leaders make a difference in their organizations and in their member's values and pastors make a difference in their churches and congregants' perspectives."[395] He states, "to help protect and enhance habits that promote cross-cultural relationships, Allport (1954) found that organizational support and encouragement of the leadership was important."[396]

DeYoung, after dealing with issues that arose as his own church transitioned to a multicultural congregation, says the leader must, above all else, "be prayed up." Things arise that are unexpected. The ministry of reconciliation can be difficult yet is rewarding. There are enough obstacles, he suggests, "to have a prayer ministry that is devoted to praying solely about race relations."[397] Prayer marked the ministry of Jesus (Luke 3:21; Mark 1:35-38). His selection of leaders was preceded by a night of prayer (Luke 6:12f). He ended his ministry here on earth in a place of prayer (Matt. 26:39). Indeed the church was launched from a prayer meeting (Acts 1, 2) and was consistently found throughout the book of Acts on its knees or raising its voice heavenward. Prayer must be central in any ministry and multicultural ministry only increases the need for it.

A leader in the church of Christ must demonstrate leadership qualities before he is "called to lead" (1 Tim. 3:1-3). A leader in a multicultural church must be a personal reconciler first.[398] Peart admonishes, "You must show your love for members of other racial and ethnic groups if you desire those you lead to do the same! You can lead people only to where you are!"[399] It was Ralph Waldo Emerson who declared, "What you are shouts so loudly in my ears I cannot hear what you say!" The leader's love for people will be tested in a multicultural environment and his response to the test will be observed.

Paul challenged his colleague Peter when he withdrew from fellowship with Gentiles under pressure from Jewish believers who were present (Gal. 2:11-14). Peter is labeled "hypocritical" by his peer when he lapses back into the Jewish tradition after having enjoyed and having expressed his freedom from dietary laws. His refusal to eat with Gentiles had more to do with the issue of reconciliation than it did a concern for Mosaic laws. Paul's challenge was "in the presence of all" because Peter's actions were sure to influence many. The incident reveals the importance of role models, the difficulty of following one's convictions and the need for leaders who are willing to confront actions that run contrary to the gospel message.

How much of any particular culture should be brought into a diverse congregation? Greer Anne Ng asks, "Why inculturate? Why try to bring into a faith community's corporate encounters with the living God forms, symbols, and music that are distinctive to particular cultures?" Her answer is, first of all, that "the incarnation is God's self-enculturation in this world."[400] Secondly, is a mission concern, that of "overcoming all stumbling blocks that the gospel might be heard."[401] Paul was willing to become like a Jew to the Jew, like one outside the law to those who were outside the law – indeed he became all things to all men that he might save some (1 Cor. 9:20-23). Native peoples who have been evangelized through the centuries have lost much of their culture since it was seen as pagan, even demonic, and therefore unacceptable to Christian theology or worship. Possibly the acceptance of and incorporation of some of their traditions may have brought greater success to the evangelistic efforts among them and less resistance to the gospel among them today.

Ng states, "One manifestation of our present efforts might therefore be perceived as a 'decolonization' of worship for those minorities culturally distinct from the Euro-Anglo majority, whereas, on the part of those within the majority tradition, a manifestation might be to 'receive the gifts' of these minorities into the existing 'ordo' and rubric and song."[402] BarbaraWilkerson describes the experience of one church struggling with a transition. To assist in this transition they stressed four essentials – training for leadership, a diverse style and form of worship, religious education aimed at promoting Christian community beyond Sunday-morning settings, and outreach through projects that create bonds between people of diverse backgrounds.[403]

After considering a multitude of practical concerns and responses, one needs to understand the church's monumental challenge. Peart comments,

> The historical failure of the evangelical church in America to make the ministry of racial reconciliation a central component of its purpose is now limiting its ability to release the gospel's power to heal racial divisions. The church must not only attempt to bring estranged people together but must also deal, as only the church can, with the issues that separated them. To do less is to create a cosmetic truce, a truce that is acknowledged but not applied. Such an approach covers up the issues, hoping that they will go away, but this approach cannot deal with the resultant damage brought about by centuries of abuse, hurt and anger.[404]

Peart goes on to enumerate the ways that black-white relations are debilitated: obstructive traditions, a sense of superiority or inferiority, lack of trust, and false sense of self-sufficiency.

How do we get people to face the issue of racism and to see themselves honestly when it comes to race issues? Ng says majority congregations "need to learn cultural aware-ness including their own 'invisible, weightless, knapsacks of cultural imperialism' that must be unpacked. These churches need to affirm each person's cultural heritage and teach atti-tudes of respecting and appreciating other cultures."[405] A group that wishes to promote genuine racial reconciliation may lay down a foundation through surveys, training and focused discussion.[406] Ng encourages various means to pro-mote people's ability to listen as carefully, truly and deeply as possible to their neighbors. She suggests,

> Our society is structured to provide as few opportuni-
> ties as possible for authentic, mutual, committed rela-
> tionships to develop across racial lines. It takes work to
> build such cross-cultural friendships. I have found that
> my most lasting and satisfying bicultural relationships
> have not been easy. They have required intentionality.
> They have been painful at times. I have cried deeply
> over disagreements, mutual challenges and my own
> racism. But I have also laughed long and hard . . . and
> felt strongly affirmed when with those friends.[407]

She then concludes, "All we are asked to do is to stop looking for easy answers to the problem of racism . . . easy attempts at racial reconciliation. Beyond easy there is work."[408]

Ray Bakke appeals to the churches in North America to embrace the cities and to celebrate the diversities found there as God's gifts.[409] The embrace of diversity requires the "explicit commitment to becoming a new kind of faith community – one that celebrates the gifts of diversity in the ways the group worships God and serves its neighbors."[410] Is the church to wait to deal with the crises that multicultural ministry might raise or is it to proactively investigate the multicultural resources within our reach so that an appropriate response may be formulated to deal with the changing demographics of our culture? Wilson says, "Today we have unparalleled opportunities to build intentionally and actively, a culture of pluralism among the people of many cultures. . . . If we can succeed, this is the greatest form of lasting leadership we can offer to the world."[411]

(5) Is it necessary?

The Imperative of the Gospel

Sheppard and Worlock write, "The Church is to be a sign of the unity of those who believe in Christ. It cannot be a faithful sign if it is itself divided and torn apart."[412] Peart says, "There is an integral link between racial reconciliation and spiritual reconciliation. Racial reconciliation must not be seen as a rival to evangelism or discipleship but an outgrowth of the gospel."[413] It must be linked to salvation for the following reasons:

> Christians must pay attention to the important premise in the Bible that God's actions stand as patterns for the actions of his people. The believer's understanding of reality should be governed by God and not by the culture around him or her. The gospel is evidenced and magnified by the actions of its adherents.[414]

Reconciliation is an integral part of the gospel. The two cannot be separated, for the gospel is reconciliation. Reconciliation is not a rival to the gospel. It is a result of God's saving work. It is not an option for believers but a necessity for those submitted to the Lordship of Christ. There is a unity in the gospel that transcends all divisions. Racial reconciliation is God's desire and cannot be set apart from spiritual reconciliation. The greatest dividers of humanity (race, gender, class, nationality) are made inconsequential by the greatest Uniter of humanity – Christ Jesus.[415]

The church's evangelistic and discipleship ministries must include encouragement, and rebuke if necessary, for new and older Christians to live out the racial unity that is a reality in Christ. This calls for a total reevaluation of the norms in society and a willingness to walk counter to the world when necessary. In God's reality racial reconciliation is attainable because Christ has already removed all barriers except one – our choices. He has made racial reconciliation, as He has our spiritual unity, a positional reality. Unfortunately the experiential unity for many ethnicities has not equaled the positional unity they have in Christ.

The ministry of racial reconciliation should be linked to the gospel because the behavior of Christians is evidence of and magnifies the truth of the gospel. Newbigin says,

> How is it possible that the gospel should be credible, that people should come to believe that the power which has the last word in human affairs is represented by a man hanging on a cross? I am suggesting that the only answer, the only hermeneutic of the gospel is a congregation of men and women who believe it and live by it. I am of course, not denying the importance of the many activities by which we seek to challenge public life with the gospel – evangelistic campaigns, distribution of Bibles and Christian literature, conferences, and even books such as this one. But I am saying that these are all secondary, and that they have the power to accomplish their purpose only as they are rooted in and lead back to a believing community.[416]

Rivers remarks, "God has called us to a challenge, and the integrity of our witness before the world hangs in the balance."[417] It must be more than hugging and crying, beating one's chest and "howling at the moon," as sometimes evidenced at Promise-keeper gatherings. If all of this is done "in the absence of the truth, in the absence of justice, in the absence of compassion and forgiveness, then we are living a lie."[418] Rice and Perkins encourage action, "Once we've sincerely admitted that we have fallen short of God's will for black and white, and after we've put the problem before the only Physician who can heal us, we must move from conviction and passion to action."[419] What would happen if churches around the world were known as places of such great love that the boundaries of culture, class, and color were shattered?

The Spiritual Dimension

Many Christian authors point to the nature of this struggle as being a spiritual one. We are "wrestling not against flesh and blood but against principalities and powers." Rivers says that there must be an understanding that this spiritual problem is "mediated through mechanisms of domination that have institutionalized themselves and reproduced themselves at every level of this society."[420] He points to how deeply entrenched these racist attitudes are. Racism is the "mediating lens through which social reality is itself framed in this society."[421]

He brings us back to our founding as a nation to recognize that we were "born in sin and shaped in iniquity." This nation began with a fundamental contradiction. Its founders affirmed "all men are created equal" while subjecting one segment of its population to the indignities of slavery. C. Eric Lincoln states:

> The American Commonwealth, which was conceived in liberty for some, was born in slavery for others. . . . As a nation, we were conceived in the most patent of political contradictions. We asserted that all men were created equal, with certain inalienable rights, as we casually stripped vast numbers of Africans of every vestige of their rights.[422]

While the institution of slavery was eradicated through a bloody conflict, the underlying assumption of white supremacy has never been rooted out. This is the demonic ideology, Rivers suggests, that blocks America's prayers and keeps our nation from becoming what it wants to be.[423]

Solutions must be forthcoming on both sides. Rivers states that blacks must stop lying to whites. Whites must recognize their own prejudice as well as seeing the different forms of racism (including "metaracism" where a social system takes on a life of its own).[424] Rivers comments, "ten million black people face a crisis of catastrophic proportions." A simple but telling statement is that "the only hope that this country has is for the church to become in fact the body of Christ."[425] He challenges white Christians to expand the parameters of their thinking that God might "free them from their whiteness" so they might "live a more saved life, free from oppression to their own demonic conceptions of what counts for beauty and human nature."[426]

Ron Potter points out that the most comprehensive study on race relations in the U.S. in this century, done by the Swedish social scientist Gunnar Myrdal, has for the most part, been ignored by the church. Myrdal summarizes "the American dilemma" as "the conflict and contradiction between biblical and democratic principles of justice, freedom and equality and the realities of racial injustice, discrimination and inequality."[427] Potter goes on to frame this crisis in terms of the history of the evangelical response. Carl Henry, in the late 40's, called for conservative Protestants to engage their social environment, something that had been ignored by Fundamentalists through the 20's and 30's. His pivotal question was this: "Is evangelicalism's only message today the proclamation of individual rescue from a foredoomed generation? Or has this evangel implications also for the most pressing social problems of our day?"[428] Yet even as he posed this question, he and other evangelical leaders evaded the issue of race, the "American dilemma." Several contemporary evangelical theologians are named who likewise have offered scant reflection on the issue of racism. An examination of several ethics books written by Evangelicals found that few mentioned or addressed the issue of race. Rivers quotes Cone's criticism of the white theological establishment: "white theologians are still secure in their assumptions that important theological issues emerge out of the white experience."[429]

Finally, William Willimon reminds us that this goal of a church gathered from all the nations can only be a miracle of God as it was at Pentecost. The waiting and praying of the disciples there signified their utter dependency. He says,

> The next move must be solely up to God, something like the resurrection itself. Empowerment will come as a gift, as a miracle, not through their efforts. Their challenge is not to become more conversant in the thought patterns of other cultures, but rather to be more exclusively tethered to their Risen Lord. What they are asked to do is not a strategy for church growth but rather the cultivation of a sense of dependency upon God to work for them what they cannot.[430]

He calls the church to be the church firmly stating, "The world is changed, not by appeal to allegedly universal categories like 'humanity,' 'love,' or 'inclusiveness,' but rather by God's election of a particular people, in a particular place and time, to be a blessing to all the peoples of the world."[431]

It was obvious in the early church that the inclusion of the Gentiles was:

> so odd, so against the grain of Israel's conventional theological thinking, that nothing less than a miracle could explain so odd a lurch toward such offensive people as Cornelius, Agrippa, and the Ethiopian. Nothing less than the miracle of Acts 2 can explain

such a move. The Gentiles are present, not through any appeals to so limp a virtue as 'inclusivity,' but rather through the leading, prodding, and gift of the Spirit. Even as the gospel rests upon the miracle of the res- urrection, so the church's inclusive proclamation rests upon the miracle of Pentecost.[432]

Willimon suggests that too much of the church's current thinking about multiculturalism is "infected with the thought of the old world and proceeds as if nothing has changed, as if the means and methods of the old world are still intact, still able, through some earnest strategy, or appeal to allegedly universal values, to bring people together despite our differ- ences." The power of Pentecostal preaching must let go of the world's hopes for community through the world's devices. Pentecost, he says, is a purifying fire judging godless hopes for human unity. Pentecost is also a sign of fulfillment, "a sign of the miraculous inclusion of 'all flesh' into the election of Israel." Thus he says, "it is quite natural for us to think of Acts 2 as a supremely 'multicultural text' for the church . . . in Jesus, all have been saved and, at Pentecost, we see God's dramatic determination to have all."[433]

Willimon's comments seem to challenge much of what has been dealt with above. If it is not a contradiction, it is cer- tainly a word of caution and balance. He says, "According to Acts 2, cross-cultural communication does not need better technique or greater sensitivity to and appreciation of our cultural differences. Cross-cultural hearing and comprehension is possible because God wills to make a way when, humanly speaking, there is no way."[434] He warns that churches that talk a great deal about diversity generally have little of it; those that speak of multiculturalism, as opposed to those that speak of evangelism tend to be the most homogeneous.

He cautions us that the gospel is "deferential and accommodating to no particular culture; rather it is indoctrination, inculcation into a new and oddly based culture, namely the church."[435] At Pentecost the linguistic divisions of Babel are healed. "The same God who scattered the nations in order to prevent a united nations against God, now gathers and unites the nations, in a new nation convened by God. The church is a sign on earth of what heaven wants."[436] The speech of Pentecost was miraculous. The hearing was also miraculous as three thousand heard the gospel and repented. The gospel was heard and embraced, forming a new family. Willimon holds forth this powerful challenge,

> Throughout Acts, the church is that (often reluctant) people who are being pushed out into confrontation with and address of other peoples (8:27-29; 10:17-20; 11:12; 13:2,4). The gospel is inherently cross-cultural, confrontive, inevitably conflicted with every cultural enclave, including the very first culture in which it found itself. Apostles in Acts will talk with anyone, even Gentiles. . . . It is the nature of the gospel to be loquacious, evangelistic, and eager to speak with anyone who

will listen. . . . the predominant imperative produced by Easter is, 'Go! Tell!' (Mk. 16:7). . . . throughout Acts, after Pentecost, the Word triumphs, overcomes all barriers, spreads like wildfire throughout the Empire. One of the great joys of the preaching ministry is to be able to witness the rather miraculous ability of the Holy Spirit to grant, in our listeners, a hearing, a response that is not of our devising, a response that is better than our preaching. . . . To preach with the Holy Spirit is to be out of control, to allow our church to be dragged kicking and screaming into encounters with cultures not our own. . . . the story seems to go out of its way to insist that any mission across cultural boundaries is due, not to our sensitivity to and savvy working of cultural differences but rather to the insistent prod of the Holy Spirit . . . whenever by the grace of God our preaching overcomes some cultural boundary, we are right to rejoice that God continues to work wonders through the word.[437]

He concludes, very appropriately, "Whenever we hear 'multicultural' we are supposed to think 'church,' that peculiar cross-cultural people gathered by nothing other than the descent of the Holy Spirit."[438] Amen to that.

CHAPTER FOUR

FINDINGS FROM THE RESEARCH AND RESPONSES

(೧ ೧)

The purpose of my Doctor of Ministry project was to identify key factors that facilitate the attendance and assimilation of minorities into majority or multicultural congregations (MCC) rather than a church of their own ethnicity. The stated hypothesis was: there are key factors that may be identified which lead minorities to attend and assimilate into majority or multicultural congregations. The project sought to discover if these identifiable factors would emerge from questionnaires and ranking sheets given to congregants (rather than to pastors and professional staff). The project sought to discover if this approach would give results different than those found in the literature and particularly with research done with church leaders. The responses received were from those who actually had the experience of leaving an ethnic church, of which they had been a part for quite a number of years (some for their entire lifetime), and entering a church of another ethnicity or race or one that was very integrated.

As a pastor of a very diverse congregation, including now some seventy different nationalities, I have repeatedly been asked the question, "How did this come about?" Most pastors and laymen recognize how unique a phenomenon this is in the United States even if they have never seen the statistics or read the literature. It was my intention to find out from those who have begun to attend a MCC, most of them having attended an ethnic church for many years, what was instrumental or critical in their making this transition. In a survey done at GGF in the fall of 2006 it was determined that the overwhelming majority (66%) of minorities attending had been part of an ethnic church for more than ten years. Over half (53%) had attended an ethnic church for fifteen years or more and more than one third (36%) for over twenty years. The question was, "What had caused them to make a transition to a basically homogeneous white church (years ago) or a multicultural church (for those who had come more recently)?" In order to answer the questions posed by many, I did not want to rely on my own perceptions or on the perceptions of other pastors and church leaders but I desired to find out firsthand what was the motivation behind such a decision and what obstacles were encountered in the process.

Prior Research

Results are compared with those published by George Yancey as part of a study funded by the Lilly Foundation (2003).[439] To reiterate, the factors that had emerged from Yancey's study querying pastors and church leaders identified the following seven factors as of major significance in growing a MCC: inclusive worship, diverse leadership, an overarching goal, intentionality, location, personal skills and adaptability.

Yancey arrived at these seven factors through a process beginning with a national telephone survey of people who went to racially integrated churches. From these individuals a random list of multicultural congregations was composed. A nationwide mail survey then was sent to these multicultural congregations. Pastors, priests or other leaders of congregations filled out the questionnaire. They were asked to check off reasons why their church had become multicultural. Eighteen possible answers were supplied. This led to a factor analysis that "indicated that there were four basic explanations for the origin of multiracial churches."[440] The eighteen variables were assigned to one of these four explanations generated by the factor analysis. Visits and interviews followed the mail survey and the responses given led Yancey to the seven general principles given above. A follow-up survey helped to "identify which of the seven principles each church utilized and implemented in the life of their congregation."[441]

The explanations were grouped under the following four categories of churches: Leadership, Evangelism, Demographic and Network Multicultural Churches. A Leadership MCC results from the leadership skills and vision of the clergy, laity or both. Members of these churches are very willing to follow the direction of leaders and make necessary changes to become a MCC. The majority of these churches are Charismatic according to Yancey's findings. The Evangelism MCC becomes integrated by winning members of other races to Christ. Whether they specifically target minorities or whether they simply "cast a wide net" they catch a wide variety of "fish." These churches tend to be conservative and fundamental. Demographic MCC's are those churches that go through a transition because of the changes in the surrounding neighborhood. Often these are churches that are in transition and they may not remain multicultural. They tend to be the more liberal congregations theologically. The last type of church Yancey mentions is the Network MCC. These churches grow through multiracial friendships, interracial marriages or integrated social settings.[442] These Network churches are the most likely to continue to grow according to Yancey's study. Apparently having a friend or relative at a church is vital for helping people gain the confidence to join.[443]

The churches fitting this model may be from any denominational or theological tradition.

In my own research some interesting, unique and rather surprising factors were identified. The implementation of the project afforded me opportunity for theological and pastoral reflection. Out of this reflection have emerged proposals for ministry implementation. Inasmuch as certain identified factors descriptive of the MCC were consistently ranked as "of great significance" I believe that the project was a qualified success. The clustering resulting from a methodology known as Multidimensional Scaling (MDS) has resulted in five distinct areas that can be identified as factors that attract minorities to a MCC. The following provides an analysis of the research data gathered during this project including conclusions drawn by the researcher. In the responses of parishioners several of the factors mentioned by Yancey consistently surfaced while others were not even mentioned. Congregants also mentioned factors that were not found among those noted by Yancey. The seven factors arrived at in Yancey's study are examined in order give a framework to the feedback and conclusions of my project.

Interpretation of Results of the Research Location

Location, one of Yancey's key "principles of successful multicultural churches," was not in the mind of the thirty attendees of GGF. Not one of them mentioned it in answer to the research question. Apparently, because of the diversity of Rockland County and the accessibility of any church in the county, location was not, in their minds, a major contributor to growing a multicultural congregation. GGF happens to be directly off a major highway running north and south in Rockland County so it is quite accessible from every part of Rockland. Obviously the factor of location might be relevant in locals where a decision to keep or to move the site of one's meeting place made it either more accessible or inaccessible to a certain population. In Rockland County there certainly are segregated neighborhoods. These segregated neighborhoods tend to be where lower socio-economic groups, often immigrants, live within older "villages." However, the majority of Rockland today consists of middle class neighborhoods, which are fairly integrated with easy accessibility to most locations in Rockland.

The significance of location has certainly been a key factor in years past as churches have made decisions to move from urban areas to suburban, from neighborhoods that were changing demographically to new and burgeoning communities. This kind of move has often been termed "white flight" and has been a source of frustration and resentment for minorities. It has made a statement that discrimination is alive and well in America and in the church of America.

This is less of a factor today where cities, communities and neighborhoods are experiencing much more diversity than in past decades. There is even a return of the more affluent and of the majority (white) population to urban areas. There are also churches today that are intentionally staying in changing neighborhoods because of a conviction that they are called to reach that neighborhood whatever ethnic group(s) might be present.

Inclusive Worship Styles and Diverse Leadership

Inclusive worship styles and diverse leadership were two factors that were consistently mentioned in the responses of the congregants as they had been in the surveys from pastors and church leaders. However, by no means, did they "top the charts" in the ranking sheets. Diverse leadership and diverse pastoral staff were ranked #26 and #28 among the forty items listed as important in a multicultural church. The mean score given was 5.95 and 5.77 (on a scale where 7.00 is most important), showing they are highly valued but behind a number of other items. The African-Americans (6.30) and Africans/ Islanders (6.11) valued diverse leadership slightly higher than the Hispanics (5.57) or the Asian participants (5.25). These were also more highly valued by the older generation (6.14 to 5.44) and by the long time attendees (6.5 to 5.73). Several authors have noted the importance of diverse leadership, particularly to African-Americans.

"Diverse worship styles" was ranked #29 of the forty items and "preachers of different ethnicities" at #31. Expressive worship was ranked significantly higher at #18. Every ethnic group rated expressive worship higher than diverse styles. The older generation rated it higher than the younger (6.62 to 5.78). This seems to indicate that styles of music are less important than "freedom of expression" in worship. Ethnic groups (particularly Blacks and Hispanics) have often felt that white congregations do not truly have this freedom. They are quite unwilling to surrender it because it is seen as integral to their worship – more so than music representing a particular ethnic flavor. For many it is seen as "Biblical." For this reason a Pentecostal or Charismatic church or fellowship of churches would seem to have an advantage in attracting minorities over churches that are less demonstrative in their worship. "Adjusting to a new worship style" was ranked as a significant obstacle particularly by African-Americans and by Hispanics. "Adjusting to a new preaching style" was more of an obstacle to the African-American attenders.

Charismatic and Pentecostal churches usually encourage the lifting of hands, the clapping of hands, and vocal, audible, even emotional and demonstrative praise. Many are open to dance and other movement such as the waving of banners.

Ethnic styles of music may be less important today to many ethnicities, especially to a second or a younger generation of believers, who are embracing contemporary Christian music. There are many styles, from gospel, to rap, to rock as well as a "worship" genre. Today these styles are, at least among young people, not necessarily identified with any particular culture or ethnicity, and are enjoyed by a cross section of cultures. The younger generation in our research ranked both diverse and expressive worship as less important than the older generation.

What was seen to be more important among the participants than the diversity of the leadership was the character and sensitivity of the leadership. The older group (those over 40) was somewhat more concerned to have diverse staff, diverse leaders and preachers of different ethnicities than were the younger attendees. Those who had begun attending GGF years ago were also more concerned about these matters. This can also be said of African-American and other blacks. The older group also particularly saw a greater need for a diversity of greeters in the church. (This may indicate the perception that the greeters do in fact convey "who is welcome in this place" to some.) They also felt somewhat more strongly the need to address racial issues and preach on the subject of race and diversity. "Prayerful leaders" was number one with every participant rating it "of great importance."

Four of the top six items of greatest importance in a multicultural congregation had to do with leadership. Absolutely essential, participants voiced, are "humble leaders," "leaders who listen" and "leaders who do not show favoritism" (mean scores of 6.75, 6.71 and 6.79).

Personal Skills

These coveted characteristics of leaders are related to the personal skills that Yancey discovered to be of vital importance yet they may be seen as in some sense different as well. Yancey had singled out "sensitivity to different needs, patience, the ability to empower others, and the ability to relate to those of different races" as necessary marks of Christian leaders.[444] He acknowledged that his list was not exhaustive. From the responses of this research there certainly are others that could be added to his list. Among the other items felt to be of greatest importance in a MCC are "acceptance regardless of color, class or race," "feeling my needs were being met and cared for" and "sensitivity of leaders to minorities." These were ranked quite high (#3, #14 and #15). "Training of leaders in cultural issues/conflict resolution" and a "willingness to learn about other cultures" were also items with an average score over 6.00 and ranking above "diverse leadership." It seems very apparent that sensitive, caring leaders are crucial to the development of a MCC.

Comparing these responses with the ranking of "obstacles" to attending a majority church one may see some of the same types of concerns expressed. Adjusting to worship or preaching styles or dealing with different political agendas all ranked below concerns that were much more on a feeling or an emotional level. Among the top ten on the list of obstacles were: "hearing hurtful, inappropriate comments" (#1), "insecurity, feeling I am different" (#3), "the question 'Will I feel significant?' " (#4), "the fear of non-acceptance or rejection" (#5), "the question 'Will the majority race understand me?' " (#6), and "dealing with stereotypes" (#7). All of these reflect either some lack of self-esteem or self-confidence or a basic insecurity or anxiety on the part of the minority person as well as a reticence to "enter the unknown." It is a natural human response when one does not know what to expect or how others will respond to us. "Dealing with unintentional ignorance" and "dealing with stereotypes" were higher concerns for blacks than for others. These expressions highlight the importance of a caring leadership and such things as "the warm, genuine welcome" (#6) on the part of members of the church as well as "a sense that one is loved and accepted regardless of class, race and color" (#3). The Asians expressed "insecurity, feeling I am different" and being self-conscious (about accents, dress, etc.) as obstacles to their attending a MCC.

Overarching Goal

The "overarching goal" spoken of by Yancey, is spoken of in different terms in several of the responses of GGF participants. The meaning units included a "mission statement including diversity" as well as a "mission statement emphasizing evangelism." The ranking showed people were significantly more concerned that such mission statements include evangelism rather than diversity. This seems to support Yancey's conclusions regarding the overarching goal. Yancey states:

> There has been a movement in the United States that emphasizes creating a multicultural nation. While many individuals accept this goal, other individuals reject multiculturalism. They are tired of extraordinary efforts to create racial diversity and believe that the best way to deal with racism is to ignore the reality of race. Whether or not Christians agree with the ideas of such individuals, it is still important to be ready to deal with them, since people with such race fatigue will most likely make up a sizeable amount of the resistance we face in maintaining a multiracial congregation. It will be these church members who will fight for the racial status quo and resist the changes that will be necessary to help convert a monoracial church into a multiracial church. Having an overarching goal is an important way to defuse the potential objections of individuals who resist changing cultural elements within a church. If being multiracial helps fulfill a goal that is important to the members of a particular church or ministry, then it becomes easier for the leaders of that church to

encourage fellow church members to put forth efforts necessary to create a multiracial ministry.[445]

Yancey goes on to say, in the light of this, that it is not wise for leaders to put the main focus on the effort to be multicultural. Rather, these efforts should be in the context of a larger goal of the church such as evangelism.[446] This seems to be in line with the sentiments of GGF participants as they rated the need for a mission statement emphasizing evangelism extremely high (#10), while a mission statement including diversity was low on the list (# 33 of 40). "Evangelism is likely to become an important overarching goal for the multiracial conservative Protestant church," according to Yancey.[447] Obviously the target of evangelistic efforts will determine how much this goal brings one closer to the ideal of a multicultural congregation. When there are "creative outreaches to ethnicities," which was a perceived need of one of the GGF participants, and ranked as somewhat important to very important by all participants, a MCC is sure to follow. When this is a priority in a church it will move that church to make changes to accommodate newcomers, changes that ensure that they will be comfortable. In conclusion, Yancey suggests:

> Sometimes a direct approach is not the best answer to a problem. A church leader can sometimes alienate church members through an overt multicultural emphasis. If church leaders desire to minimize resistance from church attendees, it is valuable for a mul-

tiracial emphasis to be tied to nonracial overarching goals. Yet racially integrated ministries also need to be intentional in their efforts to become or maintain their multiracial nature.

The challenge is not to focus on multiculturalism as the goal but to bring understanding that multicultural ministry is a means to the ultimate goal and should therefore be sought intentionally.

Intentionality

Yancey is convinced that without intentional efforts multiracial congregations will not be sustained. He concludes, backed by his research, that MCC's do not just spring up. "They are the result of intentional efforts on the part of church leaders and members to create or maintain an integrated congregation."[448] One must examine the list given by GGF participants to relate specific items to "intentionality." There are certainly any number of items that appear to fall into this category. Leaders are needed who function "without favoritism," who are "sensitive to the needs of minorities," who are "trained in conflict resolution," and who have a "willingness to learn about other cultures." All of these require intentional effort and preparation on the part of leadership.

These items, as well as "diverse leadership," are ranked in the top twenty of the characteristics of a MCC. Yancey points out how achieving a diverse leadership often takes very intentional effort on the part of the church leaders because Americans

> live in a segregated society and usually have friends and contacts of our own race. This means we tend to locate leaders who are of the same race as ourselves and have to make extra efforts to find leaders of different races. We may even have to resist hiring or appointing leaders of our own race.[449]

Diverse leadership will give minorities an assurance that their concerns and perspectives will not be ignored or neglected. A diversity of lay leadership was ranked higher than diversity of the pastoral staff (#20 versus #29). At GGF the diversifying of lay leadership happened quite quickly and naturally. Early in the 1990's the deacon board of the church consisted of three Caucasians, three Hispanics and three Blacks. These were individuals nominated by members and approved by the elders and the congregation.

However, it was more of a challenge to find minority individuals who would provide qualified pastoral leadership within contacts in our Fellowship of churches, the Fellowship of Christian Assemblies. This Fellowship began primarily among Scandinavian immigrants and has continued to be primarily white although the diversity of its congregations far exceeds the norm in America. When African Americans in the membership of GGF had expressed the need for diversity of the staff, it seemed that God sovereignly, in answer to that concern and prayer, brought a person of color who was able to fit in marvelously and serve alongside the present pastoral staff. One should not diminish the need for prayer and the need for the guidance and provision of the Holy Spirit at times like this. On the other hand, in acknowledging the sovereign work of God one also concedes the need for openness to this kind of change and the desire for it on the part of leaders. Yancey notes that racially diverse leadership is especially important in attracting African Americans.[450]

At GGF the diversity came before there was a pastor of color on staff. However, prior to the hiring of an African-American on the pastoral staff, GGF was aided in becoming a MCC by the presence an African-American musician (pianist/keyboard player) who was immensely influential in the direction and style of its worship. His involvement brought diversity in music styles, a more expressive worship style and a visible minority presence. He ministered as a truly humble servant of the Lord and a role model to many. He eventually became the full time music and arts pastor.

Once again Yancey notes, "Racially diverse leadership seems to play a role in helping promote an inclusive worship style."[451] He suggests that any attempt to reach out to a group that is especially alienated in the community should include a member of that group within the leadership structure of the church. As this discussion has demonstrated, one cannot separate factors such as diverse leadership, inclusive worship, personal skills and intentionality. Indeed intentionality seems to be an umbrella or the glue connecting the other factors.

It is interesting that "intentionality" was the factor to which Pastor Cymbala of Brooklyn Tabernacle seemed to react negatively. He seemed to express that intentionality somehow negated the work of the Holy Spirit, who is responsible to carry out the work of reconciliation among believers and who will supply the godly leaders necessary for the smooth functioning of the body. Then again, Cymbala may simply be an example of a leader who is open to change, accepting of people of different cultures, and naturally creating an environment that says "you are welcome in this place." Such an atmosphere is conducive to the building and sustaining of a MCC without a great deal of effort expended on "intentional" actions. This seemed to be the experience at GGF where intentionality was more of an afterthought subsequent to the flourishing of the multicultural dimensions of the church.

Much of the literature pointed out the need to address, rather than ignore, the issues of racism and discrimination in the church. When a sermon series at GGF touched on several related issues there was an overwhelmingly positive response from the minority population some of whom said they had never heard the issues addressed before in church. The responses of participants in this survey included "addressing racial issues" and the "preaching about diversity." This research suggests that this is of importance in the MCC.

Adaptability

The last of Yancey's factors was adaptability. He states:

> A monoracial church has only a single culture to adapt to. However, by definition, a multiracial church brings into it individuals from several different cultures. Learning how to blend these cultures together is an important part of adapting to the social reality created by the formation of a multiracial church. To this end multiracial churches have to be prepared to adapt to many new issues that will come up as different racial cultures merge together. Furthermore, the church members who have been there longer should take steps to learn more about the racial cultures of the newer members coming into the church.[452]

Openness to change was rated fairly high among GGF's participants (#16 and 6.25). This ranking did not seem to fluctuate significantly with age, ethnicity or length of time attending GGF. "The move of many churches to a contemporary worship service to accommodate the tastes of a younger cohort is one nonracial example of such adaptation," Yancey states.[453] Such responsiveness on the part of church leaders will be needed to conserve members of new racial groups. This generation is finding new ways to "do church" and this will be an important factor in ministering to a younger generation as well as to a diversity of ethnicities.

The responses from GGF's participants indicated little concern for translation into other languages. This indicates a constituency that is overwhelmingly second generation and English speaking. Obviously this concern would be much higher among first generation immigrants. How will churches address this concern in the future? New technology and additional services make it much easier to minister to a non-English speaking segment of our society rather than relegate them to a cloistered community of their own kind. Teaching English as a second language may be one of the most productive outreaches in this generation. Even the use of signage in other languages conveys respect for another culture.

Summary of Results

In review of the data, support exists for the hypothesis of this project, that key factors that lead minorities to attend and assimilate into majority or multicultural congregations may be identified. Alongside the seven factors identified by Yancey, into which many of our characteristics fit quite naturally, there is place for a few others. The Multidimensional Scaling resulted in a map with five fairly distinct clusters. The items in each of the clusters are as follows:

Cluster #1
1. Diverse worship styles
2. Expressive worship
3. Length of service (too long)
4. Length of service (too short)
25. Provision of translation
26. Celebration of ethnic holidays*
32. Outreach to ethnicities*
36. Diverse greeters
39. Advertising diversity*
*These three items shift to another cluster when six clusters are formed.

Cluster #2
5. Preaching diversity
6. Addressing racial issues
12. Leaders who listen
13. Leaders without favoritism
14. Leaders who are prayerful
27. Non-judgmental message
30. Humble leaders
31. Training for leaders in cultural issues/conflict management
37. Leaders who demonstrate concern and sensitivity for minorities
40. Bible centered preaching

Cluster #3
7. Diverse pastoral staff
8. Diverse leadership (elders, deacons, etc.)
9. Preachers of different ethnicities
22. A mission statement that includes diversity

Cluster #4
10. Cross-cultural relationships
11. Feeling my needs are met, concerns are understood, cared about
15. Family atmosphere

16. Warm welcome
17. A sense that one is loved and accepted regardless of class, race, color
21. Acceptance of interracial marriage
28. Willingness to learn about/understand other cultures
29. Opportunity for children to experience a MC environment
33. Openness to change
34. A sense that one does not have to give up his cultural uniqueness
38. Interactions inside and outside of church

Cluster #5
18. A mission-minded church
19. Involvement in missions in my home country
20. Concern for world events
23. A mission statement that is evangelistic

In this research methodology it is up to the researcher to label these clusters. The clusters were reviewed with the goal of understanding how items in a cluster were similar. Items at extreme ends of the clusters on the map were reviewed to determine how they are different. Based on this review the clusters were assigned labels as follows:

Cluster #1 – The Diverse Worship Experience

Cluster #2 – The Attitudes, Actions and Message of the Leader

Cluster #3 – A Diverse Leadership

Cluster #4 – The Opportunity for Fellowship/Relationship

Cluster #5 – A Mission-minded Congregation

Comparing these clusters/factors with Yancey's findings one finds similarities and differences. "Inclusive worship" corresponds with "The Diverse Worship Experience." "Diverse Leadership" is found in both studies. So there is obvious correlation in two main factors. "The Attitudes, Actions and Message of the Leader" corresponds to "Personal Skills" in Yancey's research. However, one might also distinguish these by suggesting that the characteristics associated with "attitudes, actions and message of the leader" are deeper and stronger character qualities than those which are related to "personal skills" in the research of Yancey. Personal skills appear to be items that one becomes proficient at through study and practice (such as understanding of cultures, learning reasons for misattribution, etc.) whereas the attitudes and actions and message of the leader refer to consistent Biblical character traits (such as humility, sensitivity, prayerfulness and love and acceptance of others).

In this research "Adaptability" was found, not as an overriding theme, but simply as one item among the meaning units ("openness to change"). "Location," as mentioned above, was not even brought up. "The Overarching Goal" is less important to our participants. This variance might be expected in a study targeting lay people versus one directed to church leaders. One might relate the category of "A Mission-minded Church" to this factor if the overarching goal is evangelism.

The Key Factor(s)

The key factor that comes to the fore in this research is what I have labeled "The Opportunity for Fellowship/ Relationship." Absent from Yancey's study with church leaders is this theme of "acceptance and relationship." In the forty meaning units gathered from the participants the prominent themes are "caring, sensitive leaders" and "welcome, accep- tance, and relationship." One sees the importance of the latter in phrases such as "acceptance regardless of color, etc." and "warm welcome" and the overwhelming and strong agree- ment with these meaning units. (Twenty-nine of thirty agreed strongly with "acceptance regardless of color;" one hundred percent of participants agreed that "a warm welcome" was a characteristic of the MCC.) Pastors queried in another part of this study checked "make sure they feel welcome" as the thing they do most to cultivate a MCC. This welcome is able to overcome many of the obstacles ranked high on the list by participants (fear of non-acceptance, insecurity, worry about feeling insignificant, feeling self-conscious, unwillingness to leave comfort zone, etc.).

I believe "The Opportunity for Fellowship/Relationship" must be acknowledged as the key factor for the MCC in the light of the responses. The participants rated the following very high: "family atmosphere" (100% agreed); "interactions inside and outside of church" (86% agreed); "cross-cultural relationships" (73% agreed). "Acceptance of interracial marriage" seems to be mandatory (96% of participants agreed) for building the MCC.

There are elements in the lists of GGF participants that should be characteristic of any and every church, multicultural or not. When these factors are present, they will help to draw people of all ethnicities. Bible centered preaching, prayerful leaders, humble leaders, a warm, genuine welcome and a mission statement emphasizing evangelism are a few examples. The first African-American couple in attendance at GGF has testified that they came and then left and then returned to GGF. They were very much aware of the barriers and were dealing with some of the "obstacles." These were significant enough for them to look elsewhere. However, when they were not able to find balanced, Biblical teaching elsewhere, they decided to return and attempt to overcome the obstacles they faced in a white church. Eventually the hospitality and welcome of one couple of the church was key for them overcoming those initial hurdles.

It would appear that the cultivation of a MCC consists of doing many of the normal and necessary things to grow any church (prayerful leaders, Bible centered preaching, etc.) but with the essential need of sensitivity on the part of leaders to the unique needs of the minority individual. Leaders who listen, who treat all alike, who are concerned and caring, who are non-judgmental in their message and yet are willing to address the hard issues of racism and discrimination - these are characteristics needed to encourage the growth and development of a MCC. A willingness to learn about other cultures is an obligation of the leader of the MCC.

As a result of the responses from participants to research questions, ranking and sorting tasks and the consolidation of these in the MDS process the following factors are suggested as the key factors in attracting minorities to a majority or multicultural church:

A Diverse Worship Experience

A Diverse Leadership

A Mission-minded Church

The Attitudes, Actions and Message of the Leader and

The Opportunity for Fellowship/Relationship.

<u>These last two were consistently rated the most significant of the key factors</u>. The ten "Characteristics of the MCC" which were ranked highest by the participants fell into these two categories.

Concluding Theological Reflections

Since the 1970's pastors and church leaders have frequently bought into the principles of the Church Growth Movement including the HUP. This has often been viewed as a formula for success. Too often, leaders have allowed a pragmatic philosophy to dominate their thinking and dictate their actions and even overrule the clear theological teaching on the New Testament church. One should be asking, not "What works?" but rather "What does God want?" and "What is honoring to Him?" If pastors and church members are able to commit themselves to the will and purpose of God at any cost then the results will be consistent with His desires. Furthermore, Christian leaders must settle questions such as: Is the goal of the local church getting people in the door or is it getting them to embrace the whole gospel including the implications of that message? How will the church truly impact the world? Will it not be through a demonstration of the gospel, showing that the Good News indeed works?

This volume has taken a look at the matter of reconciliation and seen it as essential to the gospel and to the Church's very identity. It is not simply a practice of the church; reconciliation is the very nature or the essential character of the Church. Since God is a Triune God and thus a communal being, those made in his image are meant to be communal. The Church is to offer people what they long for – relationship with God and with man – bridging every spiritual and natural barrier.

The Author of diversity has intended to use diversity to reveal more of Himself to us. In the light of this reality, God's very way of being, ministry should be transformational. Our natural tendency to stay divided, to remain with those "like us," can be altered so that we become reconcilers. God is a reconciler. He calls us not only to be reconciled to Himself but to others. He calls us to proclaim this message of reconciliation to others. Pastors and church leaders are key to making this a reality. Their attitudes, actions and message can transform the church. Taking on the role of reconcilers, our message will not only be heard but also embraced. A diverse church will be one of the most powerful proclamations and demonstrations of the power of the gospel to this age. It will literally be heaven on earth.

APPENDIX A

Recommendations for Implementation in Ministry

T he following are suggestions for implementation of the above conclusions in ministry in the local church and beyond:

1. The word "reconciliation" must be restored to its proper place of centrality in the church's teaching about the work of Christ and salvation. Reconciliation has both a vertical and an equally important, horizontal dimension. The laity of the church must understand that reconciliation with God cannot be separated from reconciliation with one's fellow man. Thinking reconciliation proceeds doing reconciliation.

2. Pastors and preachers affect the attitudes and actions of congregants. Systematic and in-depth teaching from the Word on relevant topics concerning racism and rec-

onciliation is recommended to those who desire to prepare for diversity in their church. Such a sermon series
was presented at GGF in the fall of 2006. It was wonder-
fully received and greatly appreciated with many commenting that they had been lifetime church attendees
but had never heard sermons addressing these issues.
It is my conviction that these topics must be addressed
in the church in order to truly experience the full extent
of the message of reconciliation. In order to restore trust
among peoples there must be opportunity to address
those things that have led to mistrust and division. It
might include topics and exposition of passages such as
the following:

i.   The image of God in every man (Gen. 1:26f).

ii. The diversity of mankind as part of God's will
     and purpose (Gen. 10 and 11; Acts 17:26).

iii. Our common ancestry and interracial mar-
     riage (Gen. 9:18ff).

iv. Prejudice and discrimination (Acts 10; John 4).

v.   Understanding oppression and healing the
     wounds of history (Luke 10:25ff).

vi. Breaking down the walls between people
     groups (Eph. 2:14ff).

vii. Reconciliation as a key component of the
     gospel (2 Cor. 5:16-21).

3. Small groups that come together to discuss these sermon topics and to discuss experiences of prejudice and discrimination will lead to a greater understanding of fellow-believers and the identification of sources of mistrust. The workbook published by *Promisekeepers*, written by Raleigh Washington and Glen Kehrein, will be a helpful resource as well as the study questions supplied by David Anderson. Bibliographic information is supplied in the Bibliography for both of these resources.

4. The local church should attend to the work of formulating a vision statement, or as Yancey refers to it, an "overarching goal." The goal need not be diversity in order to achieve a diverse congregation. When evangelism, service to the community and concerns for justice are part and parcel of the mission statement, these lead quite naturally to a welcoming environment for different ethnicities. An appropriate and clear mission statement will often help lead to a MCC, even though diversity is not itself the primary goal.

5. Reconciliation and diversity need to be topics that are addressed by ministers within ministerial gatherings. Racism must be recognized as a continuing problem not only in our nation and our neighborhoods but also in our places of worship. Church leaders need to be challenged to speak out about this subject that is so often

neglected in Evangelical circles. Organizations such as Promisekeepers nationally and Concerts of Prayer Greater New York regionally are facilitating this kind of dialogue.

6. Pastors and church leaders must ensure that there is dialogue within the local church on issues of diversity. The church staff and lay leadership should examine those areas that may be detrimental to the goal of diversity. Church leaders must ask the question: "What are the obstacles that minorities face when attending this particular local congregation?" Intentional efforts should be made to alleviate the impediments to diversity.

7. Leaders should be sought from among the existing minorities in the congregation. One must be careful not to put unqualified and immature people into positions of spiritual leadership but one should be intentional in equipping minorities who show promise and potential, who exhibit a call of God on their lives, and who demonstrate spiritual giftings.

8. Where there is little diversity within a local congregation, liaisons should be sought with ethnic congregations. Joint prayer meetings, united worship services and cooperative service projects with various ethnic churches will allow members to experience some of the benefits and blessings of the MCC.

APPENDIX B

METHODOLOGY OF THE RESEARCH

(๏ ๏)

Note: The following describes in detail the research methodology used to arrive at the conclusions shared above and the case for the validity of the methodology. Many readers will not be interested in the details offered here but I felt it imperative to share the methodology in order to add credibility to the findings. This section is taken directly from the Doctor of Ministry project and condensed wherever possible.

Research was not found previous to his project that had posed questions to congregants of multicultural churches or to minorities in a majority congregation regarding the obstacles experienced by minority laypersons attending such churches and the characteristics of such churches that tend to attract these minorities. Therefore, the first goal of this study was to "attend to the voices of ethnic minorities" in order to more fully understand their reasons for attending a multicultural church (MCC) or a church of another ethnicity, as well as the obstacles they faced in doing so. They were also asked to identify the advantages of attending a homogeneous or ethnic congregation versus the benefits of attending a MCC.

Since this study endeavored to increase knowledge related to multicultural churches in America today, a relatively new methodology entitled Concept Mapping was utilized. This methodology combines both qualitative and quantitative research strategies. According to Darcy, Lee, and Tracey:

> Several leaders in multicultural research have under-scored the importance of nontraditional methods of inquiry to explore multicultural concerns (Fuertes, Bartolomew & Nichols, 2001; Helms, 2002; Ponterotto, 2002; Ponterotto & Alexander, 1996). They argue that reliance on traditional quantitative methods and defi-nitions of individual differences may limit the under-standing of multicultural concerns. . . . Seeking to expand the range of approaches used to explore multi-cultural issues, some researchers call for the use of less traditional quantitative methods (e.g. Helms, 2002), whereas others champion more qualitative methods (e.g., Ponterotto, 2002), which eschew the common normative definition of individual differences.[454]

Although there is disagreement over whether a qualitative approach to research in a Doctor of Ministry project is appro-priate, the researcher chose this approach with the intent of discovering factors beyond those discussed in the literature. Myers suggests three possible research methods for these projects: 1) the quantitative which attempts to measure by controlled experiments and contrasting sets of variables, ultimately arriving at objective proof; 2) the ethnographic, that sets out to understand by describing what can be seen, and 3) the pro-active or qualitative, that attempts to transform. The qualitative approach, according to Myers, "relies upon observation, interviewing, journaling and the use of documents. It is not coincidental that these skills also lie at the heart of ministerial training."[455]

Qualitative research has often been seen as having less value than the quantitative "pure" form of research. However, in many disciplines today the value of qualitative research is being appreciated and gaining wider acceptance. This researcher has read numerous studies in the Journal of Counseling Psychology and related periodicals using the methodology of concept mapping for the advantages it offers for certain types of research. Cartledge observes:

> Quantitative research has been traditionally understood to view its perspective as from the outside looking in, with detached scientific objectivity. It starts with theories and concepts that are formulated as hypotheses and tested through reliable instruments of measurement. Its procedures are logical, structured and replicable, giving rise to its law-like findings . . . it regards its data as hard, rigorous, and reliable.

Qualitative research, by contrast, does not have a fleeting or non-existent contact with the people under study, but a sustained engagement. It seeks to get close to the data and engages with the subject as an insider . . . Good and varied data can be shown to provide insights that are a rich, deep and meaningful . . . *it is widely recognized that qualitative research is not a second-rate approach.*[456]

Qualitative research can be described as exploratory and inductive, using unknown variables, and being flexible, as seen by the following description of the process. It has the possibility to build theory rather than simply test it. Its data comes from small groups through personal interviews and includes a more personal dimension. It can reduce the influence of the researcher's predispositions and bias on the conclusions.

The methodology used in this research, namely "Concept Mapping," was used to explore the phenomenon of minorities being attracted to and assimilating into majority and MCC. This methodology consisted of qualitative components – questionnaires and interviews, and also summarized the results in quantitative measurements. Concept mapping is:

a specific type of structured conceptualization process for exploring and describing the underlying structure of specific phenomena. Trochim (1989c) described concept mapping as combining thought listing, item reduction and sorting to allow participant responses to be organized meaningfully. This method has the advantage of reducing researcher bias as it asks participants to generate and organize data based on their own perspectives rather than respond to statements generated by the researcher.[457]

Concept mapping is a methodology that provides for a great deal of flexibility both in the types of data collected and in the number of stimuli needed.[458] When using concept mapping "participants are involved throughout the process of gathering and analyzing data (Davison et al., 1986; Tracey et al., 2003)."[459] According to Borgen and Barnett, concept mapping involves three steps: (1) participants express their ideas, thoughts, or experiences about a specific question or topic either orally or in writing; (2) participants engage in an unstructured card sort where they group together their ideas, thoughts, or experiences; and (3) the data collected by means of the card sorting task is analyzed using multidimensional scaling (MDS) and cluster analysis.[460]

The researcher first investigated the private phenomenological worlds of participants and then organized their feedback through the use of statistical analysis. Open-ended questions and interviews were used so that participants would not be constrained in their responses by a limited set of predetermined options chosen beforehand by the researcher or suggested by the literature. According to Paulson, Truscott and Stuart, "The use of open-ended questions allows for a broader range of responses and for the discovery of variables not previously considered."[461] When using concept mapping, researcher bias is controlled both in the manner in which the data is collected and is processed. Johnson suggests, "The use of concept mapping allows salient dimensions to emerge from the data during the process of analysis rather than being imposed a priori (Buser, 1989; Gol & Cook, 2004)."[462] She adds,

> Concept mapping is viewed as an appropriate methodology to use when the objective is to increase understanding of variables as they are perceived or understood by individuals or groups of individuals (Paulson, Truscott, & Stuart, 1999; Tracey, Lichtenberg, Goodyear, Claiborn, & Wampold, 2003; Trochim, 1989). Results obtained using this method can be confirmatory (appear in a manner proposed by theory) or exploratory (suggestive of variables needing further research and confirmation across a broader sampling of participants) (Strauss & Corbin, 1990).[463]

Borgen and Barnett summarize the advantages of one aspect of concept mapping, namely clustering:

> Three major purposes for clustering can be delineated: exploration, confirmation, and simplification . . . cluster analysis is most often used as an exploratory technique. If the research area is relatively new, clustering may be a productive early step to identify and structure the subgroups that are of potential value in understanding the research problem. . . . If prior knowledge or theory suggests a particular psychological classification, clustering might be used to test the classification. . . . Clustering can be an especially powerful technique for simplifying a complex data set.[464]

Results of this project may be both confirmatory (agreeing with the literature) and exploratory (suggesting areas for further study). It is hoped that this project results in an instrument that might be helpful in further pursuing this type of research.

Concept mapping uses the following elements: multidimensional scaling (MDS) to identify underlying dimensions, cluster analysis to identify themes, and a ranking task to understand the importance of statements for participants, both individually and as a group.[465] Feedback from participants is analyzed using multidimensional scaling which produces a cluster map that in turn provides a visual representation of the data. Buser sums up the idea behind multidimensional scaling in these words:

> Multidimensional scaling procedures are statistical techniques that uncover the 'hidden structure of data' (Kruskal & Wish, 1978). They enable one to examine the relationships among a set of stimuli when the meaningful structure underlying the relationships is unknown. In other words, the relationships and their meaning are discovered during the analysis rather than being imposed a priori.[466]

Fitzgerald and Hubert state, "Multidimensional scaling is a general term for a set of procedures that can be used to represent spatially the interrelationships among a set of objects."[467]

Davison, Richards and Rounds state, "Four steps are required in designing any MDS study: sampling participants and stimuli, choosing an appropriate data collection technique, selecting one of several MDS analyses, and interpreting the output."[468] The first step is to select participants. In this study minorities who began to attend GGF before it was a mixed congregation ethnically were chosen together with others who began to attend after it had become a very diverse congregation. The second step is to determine the type of data that will be collected from the participants. Four open-ended research questions were presented to the parishioners in order to gather and examine factors not advanced by the researcher or suggested by the literature.

Though MDS shares similarities with factor analysis, some believe it is superior if the objectives are to identify unknown variables and to represent those variables in a simple and clearly understandable manner. Johnson states, "Another advantage of using MDS is that the dimensions or structure that emerge from the data are not dependent on the rater. Therefore, this approach is seen as more closely reflecting the cognitive structure of participants. MDS allows the researcher to visually and statistically identify the significance of differences discovered." [469]

Research Questions

The following research questions were developed with a view to fulfilling the purposes of this study:

1. What obstacles do you believe individuals face (have to overcome) in making the choice to attend a church that is not one of their own race/ethnicity or in attending a multicultural church?
2. What do you believe are the most important characteristics of a church that is attracting people of various ethnicities? That is, how can a church make this transition a relatively easy one?
3. What benefits are there for individuals who attend an ethnic congregation (that of their own ethnicity)?
4. What benefits are there for individuals who attend a multiethnic congregation?

The questions were designed to be broad and open-ended to test the hypothesis and in an effort to address gaps in the literature on this issue and the need for theory-based research. This allowed the researcher to explore the phenomenological world of the average churchgoer and to gain an understanding of how they viewed their experience in attending a majority or a MCC. Participants were encouraged to provide as many answers to these questions as appropriate. The answers would be summarized in "meaning units" and participants would then rate them as to their importance. Answers would either confirm the factors put forth in the literature or would offer alternative explanations. It was also recognized that the responses could indicate that there were no clear-cut "answers," that is, no factors were consistently proffered as to why minorities were attracted to multicultural congregations. The hypothesis of this study was subject to modification based on the data gathered.

Participants

Participants were recruited from the membership roles of GGF. They were all members of an ethnic minority (African-American, African, Islanders, Hispanic, and Asian), males and females, between the ages of twenty-one and sixty-three. A total of thirty individuals were asked to participate based on the following criteria: ten of the individuals began attending GGF (at that time New City Gospel) twenty years ago when it was a "homogeneous" congregation (over 97 percent Caucasian) and twenty began attending more recently when it was an extremely diverse, multiethnic congregation (at least 50 percent ethnic minorities). Participants were selected in this manner in order to determine whether the responses varied between those who entered a homogeneous congregation as opposed to a multicultural congregation.

Studies using concept mapping and multidimensional scaling (MDS) vary in the number of subjects used. Gol and Cook note, "Most studies using MDS or concept mapping use fewer than 20 participants, in part because of the relatively large amounts of investigator effort needed for data analysis (cf. Schiffman, Reynolds, & Young, 1981)."[470] The ability to generalize findings necessitates including a number large enough to be considered a representative sample of the population being explored.

Ethical Considerations

Participants were informed of the purposes and risks associated with participating in this study and assured of their right to withdraw at any point. The confidentiality and anonymity of participants has been protected as much as is possible.

Judges

Following procedures espoused in previous concept mapping studies, a team of two judges was designated to condense information collected during the first round of data gathering, and to review the development of ranking and sorting statements. This process provides for greater objectivity in data analysis.

Measures

Packets distributed to potential participants included (1) a letter explaining the purpose of the study and requesting participation, (2) an informed consent form, (3) a brief questionnaire seeking background information and a questionnaire comprising the research questions. Participants were requested to return the questionnaire within two weeks.

Questionnaire

A questionnaire, consisting of two sections, was included in the initial packet. The first section gathered general information on the participant. The second section contained the four research questions.

Data Collection

The first step in concept mapping is to gather "ideas, thoughts, or experiences from participants related to the topic under exploration"[471] To accomplish this task two distinct data-gathering sessions were scheduled. During the initial round of data gathering, information was obtained through the use of the questionnaire and phone interviews. The second round consisted of a ranking task and a sorting task.

Meaning Units

The data from the research questions was then reviewed to identify and clarify "intrinsic meaning units." Two judges jointly analyzed the first set of data. According to Paulson, the purpose of this step "is to distill an inclusive set of statements that capture the essence of the participants' experiences, while retaining their language."[472] The judges identified key elements in the responses of participants and then restated those responses in short meaning units. The procedure and criteria to determine these meaning units were: (1) actual statements of participants were reviewed by each judge individually and the essence of that statement was expressed as succinctly as possible, (2) these expressions were compared by the judges, (3) item reduction was carried out by eliminating redundancies and nonsensical statements, and by deleting statements that did not answer the questions directly or were too vague,[473] (4) similar statements were combined into single representative statements, and (5) statements that reflected the main ideas were identified and condensed into brief meaning units. The use of judges to analyze the data helps to reduce researcher bias and enhances the reliability and validity of the findings.[474] The statements were entered on ranking sheets in three categories (the obstacles one faces in attending a multicultural congregation, the characteristics of a multicultural church that attracts minorities, and the value of a multicultural congregation). The statements that related to "characteristics of a multicultural church that attracts minorities" were then recorded on separate cards. Each card contained only one meaning unit. The entire stack of cards was referred to as a data set.

Sorting Task

The second round of data gathering included a sorting task and a ranking task. To accomplish the sorting task, each participant was sent a data set, a group of small, empty envelopes, a large stamped, return envelope, and specific instructions on how to conduct a card sort. The instructions for completing the task did not specify any criterion to use in sorting the cards. The participant was asked to determine the criterion to use to sort the cards.

Ranking Task

Together with the data set, each participant received ranking sheets in order to complete the ranking task. The ranking sheets contained a list of all meaning units generated from the data followed by a seven-point ranking scale. Instructions on how to proceed were included.

Data Analysis

Data analysis, using concept mapping methodology, occurred in the following sequential steps. First, the responses to the questionnaires were analyzed in order to extract a set of statements that most clearly depicted the thoughts and experiences of those responding. During this initial step, the analysis of written responses and typed transcripts allowed the formation of 'meaning units.' The answers for three of the research questions were placed on ranking sheets. Next, the meaning units for the first question were placed on individual cards, compiled into a data set. The ranking and sorting tasks became the second step of data collection. Information generated from the sorting task was utilized to create a matrix for each sort. These were combined into a master matrix that was then analyzed using MDS and cluster analysis from SPSS software. The clusters were analyzed to find more general "factors." Next, information collected through the use of ranking tasks was analyzed to determine the importance of the meaning units for participants. Lastly, similarities and differences between the responses of ethnic groups, age groups and the groups who began attending GGF years ago, versus more recently, were compared.

Rationale

The research question of this doctoral project has driven the methods used to collect and analyze the data.[475] The question, "Are there identifiable factors that characterize the church that is becoming multicultural?" necessitates a methodology that includes a relational component between the researcher and the participants. The primary method of gathering data has been through questionnaires and, when necessary to clarify responses, personal interviews. The methodological approach of this project correlated with the values described in the Biblical-Theological focus, as well as the insights discovered in the Review of Related Literature (The Controversy). A qualitative research approach is compatible with the type of information generated. The questions of this research project were designed to directly test the hypothesis stated.

Emerging from the initial questionnaire and from the ranking and sorting tasks should be factors that are consistently seen as being important to those minorities who participated. If the exercise reveals little or no consistency in the responses of participants, then the hypothesis of the author is not supported. In accordance with the principles of qualitative research, the hypothesis of the study must be subject to revision based on the data gathered in the study. If identifiable factors emerge from the research, it will be of great significance to compare these results with other research that has focused on the responses of church leaders rather than of lay people.

The limitations of the methodology employed are apparent. Participants must be willing to answer questions honestly and freely. There may be reasons why respondents would hesitate to be completely truthful and candid in their responses. Their relationship with the researcher may cause them to "hold back" certain information and feelings. Their understanding of the questions might be different from what the researcher intended. The researcher's understanding of the responses might be flawed (using a second "judge" has helped to ameliorate this weakness). Cultural differences may cause some disparity in the understanding and perspectives of questions and answers. The disadvantages of this methodology must simply be granted and kept in mind by the researcher and the reader.

Table 1

Most Important Characteristics of a MCC

	N	Minimum	Maximum	Sum	Mean
prayerful leaders	30	7	7	210	7.00
Bible centered preaching	30	6	7	209	6.97
acceptance regardless	30	5	7	208	6.93
leaders w/o favor	30	5	7	203	6.77
humility of leaders	30	6	7	202	6.73
leaders listen	30	5	7	201	6.70
warm welcome	30	5	7	200	6.67
family atmosphere	30	5	7	198	6.60
opportunity for children to learn	30	4	7	197	6.57
accept interracial marriage	30	4	7	194	6.47
mission statement–evangelism	30	4	7	194	6.47
sensitivity of leaders	30	4	7	193	6.43
expressive worship	30	3	7	191	6.37
mission minded church	30	4	7	191	6.37
train leaders in conflict resolution	30	4	7	190	6.33
openness to change	30	4	7	189	6.30
participation at every level	30	4	7	188	6.27
willingness to learn	30	4	7	186	6.20
needs met, cared for	30	4	7	183	6.10
non–judgmental message	30	1	7	182	6.07
not having to give up identity	30	4	7	180	6.00
diverse leadership	30	1	7	178	5.93
interactions	30	4	7	176	5.87
address rac. issues	30	1	7	175	5.83
concern for world events	30	4	7	175	5.83
outreach to ethnicities	30	4	7	174	5.80
diverse staff	30	1	7	173	5.77
cross–cult. rela	30	3	7	170	5.67
mission statement – diversity	30	1	7	169	5.63
diverse preachers	30	1	7	169	5.63
diverse worship	30	3	7	169	5.63
diverse greeters	30	1	7	167	5.57

Table 1 (Continued)

Most Important Characteristics of a MCC

	N	Minimum	Maximum	Sum	Mean
advertising diversity	30	1	7	164	5.47
missions in home country	30	2	7	158	5.27
preach diversity	30	1	7	157	5.23
service length–long	30	1	7	146	4.87
offering translation	30	1	7	124	4.13
service length–short	30	1	7	124	4.13
translation available	30	1	7	122	4.07
celebrate ethnic holidays	30	1	7	121	4.03
Valid N (listwise)	30				

Table 2

The Greatest Obstacles for Minorities Attending a MCC

	N	Minimum	Maximum	Mean	Std. Deviation
hearing hurtful, inappropriate comments	30	1	7	4.63	2.109
network of support	30	1	7	4.57	1.924
will I feel significant	30	1	7	4.50	2.146
fear of non-acceptance	30	1	7	4.47	1.889
dealing with stereotypes	30	1	7	4.40	1.793
political agendas	30	1	7	4.37	2.157
insecurity, feeling I'm different	30	1	7	4.27	1.982
culture not embraced/recognized	30	1	7	4.13	2.177
will majority race understand me	30	1	7	4.03	1.884
dealing with unintentional ignorance	30	1	7	3.97	1.938
self-conscious about accents, etc	30	1	7	3.97	2.341
concern whether children accepted	30	1	7	3.93	2.050
adjust to different worship style	30	1	7	3.87	1.655
inability to express oneself	30	1	7	3.83	2.135
fear of being judged	30	1	7	3.50	2.080
to different preaching style	30	1	7	3.47	1.871
unwilling to leave comfort zone	30	1	7	3.43	1.888
lack of familiarity with customs	30	1	6	3.43	1.455
little in common	30	1	7	3.30	1.878
not willing to give up sense of family	29	1	7	3.24	2.294
language	30	1	7	3.13	2.360
length of service	30	1	6	3.03	1.564
less likely to get involved	30	1	6	2.97	1.712
mistrust of other ethnicity	30	1	7	2.77	1.736
difficulty in understanding differences	30	1	5	2.67	1.470
pressed into a mold	30	1	6	2.63	1.691
rejection of family for leaving	30	1	7	2.37	1.752
rejection of race for selling out	30	1	7	2.33	1.749
Valid N (listwise)	29				

Table 3

The Benefits of a MCC

	N	Minimum	Maximum	Sum	Mean
place to learn to love, bond, trust	30	6	7	205	6.83
picture of heaven	30	4	7	202	6.73
balanced Bible teaching, relevant to all	30	2	7	201	6.70
God's intention at Pentecost	30	4	7	201	6.70
realize our unity beyond race	30	4	7	195	6.50
Great Commission observed	30	4	7	195	6.50
opportunity for children	30	3	7	193	6.43
cross-cultural relationships	30	2	7	193	6.43
preparation for a multicultural society	30	3	7	193	6.43
understand oneself, biases	30	5	7	192	6.40
learn to appreciate different worship style	30	4	7	191	6.37
place to understand/accept other cultures	30	4	7	191	6.37
place to dispel stereotypes	30	4	7	190	6.33
helps one become well-rounded	30	4	7	189	6.30
recognize commonalities/ similarities	30	2	7	188	6.27
see God in a different way	30	3	7	187	6.23
opportunity for repentance/forgiveness	30	3	7	187	6.23
experience worship in other ways	30	4	7	186	6.20
hearing the Word unaltered by culture	30	1	7	183	6.10
place to overcome fears	30	2	7	183	6.10
equipment for evangelism	30	2	7	180	6.00
broader perspective/experience	30	1	7	173	5.77
less focus on outward appearance	30	1	7	168	5.60
Valid N (listwise)	30				

Figure 1

Multidimensional Scaling Map – Cluster Analysis

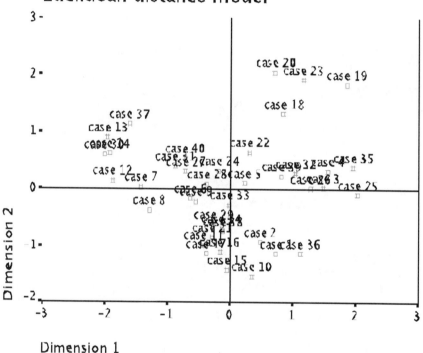

Derived Stimulus Configuration

Euclidean distance model

BIBLIOGRAPHY

Books

Adams, Jay. *The Time is at Hand*. Nutley, NJ: Presbyterian and Reformed Publishing, 1970.

Anderson, David A. *Multicultural Ministry: Finding Your Church's Unique Rhythm*. Grand Rapids: Zondervan, 2004.

Appleby, Jerry. *The Church is in a Stew*. Kansas City: Beacon Hill Press, 1990.

Bakke, Ray. A *Theology As Big As the City*. Downers Grove, IL: InterVarsity Press, 1997.

Bakke, Ray, and Jim Hart. *The Urban Christian: Effective Ministry in Today's Urban World.* Downers Grove, IL: InterVarsity Press, 1987.

Barker, Kenneth, ed. *The New International Study Bible.* Grand Rapids: Zondervan Publishing, 1995.

Barrett, C. K. *The Second Epistle to the Corinthians.* New York: Harper and Row, 1973.

Bauer, William. *A Greek-English Lexicon of the New Testament,* Translated by William F. Arndt and F. Wilbur Gingrich. Chicago: The University of Chicago Press, 1957.

Black, Kathy. *Culturally Conscious Worship.* St. Louis: Chalice Press, 2000.

Blount, Brian K. and Leonora Tubbs Tisdale, eds. *Making Room at the Table: An Invitation to Multicultural Worship.* Louisville: Westminster John Knox Press, 2001.

Bowers, Laurene. *Becoming a Multicultural Church.* Cleveland: The Pilgrim Press, 2006.

Breckenridge, James and Lillian. *What Color is Your God? Multicultural Education in the Church.* Wheaton, IL: Victor Books, 1984.

Bruce, F. F. *The Epistle to the Galations: A Commentary on the Greek Text.* New International Greek Testament Commentary. Grand Rapids: Eerdmans Publishing, 1982.

Cartledge, Mark J. *Practical Theology: Charismatic and Empirical Perspectives.* Carlisle, Cumbria, UK: Paternoster Press, 2003.

Conde-Frazier, Elizabeth, S. Steve King, and Gary Parrett. *A Many Colored Kingdom: Multicultural Dynamics for Spiritual Formation.* Grand Rapids: Baker Academics, 2005.

Crystal, David, ed. *Cambridge Encyclopedia.* Cambridge: Cambridge University Press, 1997.

D'Souza, Dinesh. *The End of Racism: Principles for a Multiracial Society.* New York: Simon and Schuster, 1996.

DeYoung, Curtiss, Michael Emerson, George Yancey, and Karen Chai Kim. *United by Faith: The Multicultural Congregation as an Answer to the Problem of Race*. New York: Oxford University Press, 2003.

Elwell, Walter and Robert Yarbrough. *Encountering the New Testament*. Grand Rapids: Baker Academics, 2005.

Erickson, Millard J. *Introducing Christian Doctrine*. Grand Rapids: Baker Academic, 2001.

Fong, Ken Uyeda. *Pursuing the Pearl: A Comprehensive Resource for Multi-Asian Ministry*. Valley Forge, PA: Judson, 1999.

Foster, Charles. *Embracing Diversity: Leadership in Multicultural Congregations*. Bethesda, MD: The Alban Institute, 1997.

Gill, Robin. *A Textbook of Christian Ethics*. Edinburgh: T. & T. Clark, 1985.

Grudem, Wayne. *Systematic Theology: An Introduction to Biblical Doctrine*. Grand Rapids: Zondervan Publishing, 1994.

Hamm, Ken, Carl Wieland, and Don Batten. *One Blood: The Biblical Answer to Racism*. Green Forest, AR: Master Books, 2000.

Hawn, Michael. *One Bread, One Body: Exploring Cultural Diversity in Worship*. Bethesda, MD: The Alban Institute, 2003.

Hines, Samuel and Curtis DeYoung. *Beyond Rhetoric: Reconciliation as a Way of Life*. Valley Forge, PA: Judson Press, 2000.

Hirsch, Jr., E.D., Joseph F. Kett, and James Trefil. *Dictionary of Cultural Literacy*, 2nd ed. Boston: Houghton Mifflin, 1993.

Hughes, Phillip. *The Second Epistle to the Corinthians*. Grand Rapids: Eerdmans Publishing, 1962.

Hunsberger, George R. and Craig Van Gelder. *The Church between Gospel and Culture: the Emerging Mission in North America*. Grand Rapids: Eerdmans Publishing, 1996.

Ireland, David. *What Color is Your God?* Verona, NJ: Impact Publishing, 2000.

Jeter Jr., Joseph R. and Ronald J. Allen. *One Gospel, Many Ears: Preaching for Different Listeners in the Congregation.* St Louis: Chalice Press, 2002.

Keil, C. F. and F. Delitzsch. *Biblical Commentary on the Old Testament.* Grand Rapids: Eerdmans Publishing, 1971.

Kwan, K. M. *Ethnic Stratification: A Comparative Approach.* New York: The MacMillan Company, 1965.

Ladd, George E. *A Theology of the New Testament.* Grand Rapids: Eerdmans Publishing, 1993.

Lane, Patty. *A Beginner's Guide to Crossing Cultures: Making Friends in a Multicultural World.* Downers Grove, IL: InterVarsity Press, 2002.

Law, Eric H. F. *The Wolf Shall Dwell With the Lamb: A Spirituality for Leadership in a Multicultural Community.* St. Louis: Chalice Press, 1993.

_____. *Inclusion: Making Room for Grace.* St. Louis: Chalice Press, 2000.

Leedy, Paul D. and Jeanne Ellis Ormod, *Practical Research: Planning and Design.* 6th ed. Upper Saddle River, N.J.: Prentice-Hall, 1996.

Maxwell, John. *Developing the Leaders Around You.* Nashville: Thomas Nelson, 1995.

McGavran, Donald A. *Understanding Church Growth.* Grand Rapids: Eerdmans Publishing, 1980.

Merriam Webster's New Collegiate Dictionary, 10th ed. Springfield, MA: Merriam-Webster, Inc., 1997.

Myers, William R. *Research in Ministry: A Primer for the Doctor of Ministry Program.* Chicago: Exploration Press, 1993.

Neibuhr, H. R. *Christ and Culture.* New York: Harper & Brothers Publishers, 1951.

Okholm, Dennis L., ed. *The Gospel in Black & White: Theological Resources for Racial Reconciliation.* Downers Grove, IL: InterVarsity Press, 1998.

Ornguze, John. *Heaven – for Whites Only*. El Cajon, CA: Christian Service Publishers, 2000.

Ortiz, Manuel. *One New People: Models for Developing a Multicultural Church*. Downers Grove, IL: InterVarsity Press, 1996.

Park, Andrew Sung. *Racial Conflict and Healing: An Asian-American Theological Perspective*. Maryknoll, NY: Orbis Books, 1996.

Peart, Norman Anthony. *Separate No More, Understanding and Developing Racial Reconciliation in Your Church*. Grand Rapids: Baker Books, 2000.

Perkins, Spencer and Chris Rice. *More Than Equals*. Downers Grove, IL: InterVarsity Press, 1993.

Richards, Lawrence O. *Expository Dictionary of Bible Words*. Grand Rapids: Regency, 1985.

Rhodes, Stephen. *Where the Nations Meet: The Church in a Multicultural World*. Downers Grove, IL: InterVarsity Press, 1998.

Sanjek, Roger. *The Future of Us All*. Ithaca, NY: Cornell Univ. Press, 1998.

Schlesinger, Jr., Arthur M. *The Disuniting of America: Reflections on a Multicultural Society*. New York: W. W. Norton, 1991.

Stassen, Glen H. and David P. Gushee. *Kingdom Ethics: Following Jesus in Contemporary Context*. Downers Grove, IL: InterVarsity Press, 2003.

Stott, John R. W. *Our Guilty Silence*. Grand Rapids: Eerdmans Publishing, 1967.

Synan, Vinson. *The Century of the Holy Spirit: 100 Years of Pentecostal and Charismatic Renewal*. Nashville: Thomas Nelson Publishers, 2001.

Verbrugge, Verlyn. *New International Dictionary of New Testament Theology: Abridged Edition*. Grand Rapids, MI: Zondervan Publishing, 2000.

Wagner, C. Peter. *Our Kind of People: The Ethical Dimensions of Church Growth in America*. Atlanta: John Knox Press, 1979.

Wagner, C. Peter. *Strategies for Church Growth.* Ventura, CA: Regal Books, 1987.

Washington, Raleigh, and Glen Kehrein. *Break Down the Walls, Experiencing Biblical Reconciliation and Unity in the Body of Christ.* Chicago: Moody Press, 1997.

Wilkerson, Barbara. *Goals of Multicultural Religious Education.* Birmingham, AL: Religious Education Press, 1997.

Woodley, Randy. *Living in Color: Embracing God's Passion for Ethnic Diversity.* Downers Grove, IL: InterVarsity Press, 2001.

Yancey, George. *Beyond Black and White: Reflections on Racial Reconciliation.* Grand Rapids, MI: Baker Books, 1996.

_____. *One Body, One Spirit: Principles for Multiracial Churches.* Downers Grove, IL: InterVarsity Publishing, 2003.

Periodicals

Borgen, Fred and David Barnett. "Applying Cluster Analysis in Counseling Psychology Research." *Journal of Counseling Psychology* 34, no. 4 (1987): 456-468.

Brush, Silla. "The New Shape of the Nation." *U.S. News and World Report*, 2 October 2006, 46-54.

Buser, Samuel Jackson. "A Counseling Practitioner's Primer to the Use of Multidimensional Scaling." *Journal of Counseling and Development* 67, (March 1989): 420-423.

Maria Darcy, Debbiesiu Lee, and Terence J. G. Tracey. "Complementary Approaches to Individual Differences Using Paired Comparisons and Multidimensional Scaling: Applications to Multicultural Counseling Competence." *Journal of Counseling Psychology* 51, no. 2 (2004): 139-150.

Davison, M. L., P. S. Richards, and J. B. Rounds. "Multidimensional Scaling in Counseling Research and Practice." *Journal of Counseling and Development* 65, (1986): 178-184.

Dill, Ellen Renee. "Unity and Difference in the Multicultural Congregation." *The Christian Ministry*, May-June 1995, 23-25.

Eugene, Toinette M. "Multicultural Ministry: Theory, Practice, Theology." *Chicago Theological Seminary Register* 84, No 2 (Spring 1994): 1-11.

Fitzgerald, Louis F. and Lawrence J. Hubert. "Multidimensional Scaling: Some Possibilities for Counseling Psychology." *Journal of Counseling Psychology* 34, no. 4, (1987): 469-480.

Flam, Faye. "DNA Shows Links Between All Living Humans." *Journal News*, 16 April 2001, 3E.

Fortney, N. D. "The Anthropological Concept of Race." *Journal of Black Studies* 8, no. 1 (Sept. 1977): 42.

Gol, Andrew and Stephen Cook. "Exploring the Underlying Dimensions of Coping: A Concept Mapping Approach." *Journal of Social and Clinical Psychology* 23, no. 2, (2004): 155-171.

La Plante, Clara. "Who Benefits from Reconciliation?" *The Christian Ministry*, May-June 1995, 20-22.

Lloyd, Rupert. "Managing a Multicultural Congregation." *Leadership* 11 (Winter 1990): 36-39.

Maudlin, Michael G. "Now that's Multicultural." *Christianity Today* 36, Jan 13 1992, 15.

Moltmann, Jürgen. "Political Theology." *Theology Today* 27. (1971): 22.

Mott, Stephen. "Multicultural Inclusiveness in Revelation." *Christian Social Action*, (June 1993): 37.

All the World Comes to Queens, National Geographic, (September 1998).

New People – New Cultures. Ramapo College newsletter, (Spring 2002): 4.

Ng, Greer Anne. "One Faith, One Baptism—One Liturgy? Worship in a Multicultural, Multifaith Context." *Reformed Liturgy & Music* 30 no 3, (1996): 146-149.

Paulson, Barbara, Derek Truscott, and Janice Stuart. "Clients Perceptions of Helpful Experiences in Counseling." *Journal of Counseling Psychology* 46, no. 3 (1999): 318-324.

Pero, Albert. "Ministry in Multi-cultural Church." *Currents in Theology and Mission* 17 (Fall 1990): 66-68.

Ruffle, Douglas W. "Building Blocks for a Multicultural Congregation." *Quarterly Review* 13 (Fall 1993): 73-82.

Swerdlow, Joel L. "Global Culture." *National Geographic* 196:2, (August 1999): 3-7.

Tapia, Andres. "The Myth of Racial Progress." *Christianity Today* 37, October 1993, 18-20.

Whalley, W. E. "The Inner City Church in a Multicultural Environment." *The Baptist Quarterly* 33, (Jan 1989): 43-50.

Willimon, William. "Everyone Whom the Lord Our God Calls: Acts 2 and the Miracle of Pentecost Preaching in a Multicultural Context." *Journal for Preachers* 25, no 4, (Pentecost 2002): 3-9.

Wilson, Henry S. "Multicultural Christian Community: A Bouquet of Multicultural Flowers." *Word and World* 24, no. 2, (Spring 2004): 172-181.

Other

B. G. Breems, "I Tell Them We Are A Blessed People: An Analysis of Ethnicity By Way of a Canadian Dutch-Calvinist Community" Ph.D. diss., University of British Columbia, 1991.

Encarta World English Dictionary, Microsoft, Bloomsbury Publishing Plc., 1999.

Crabb, Larry. *When the Leader Gets in the Way.* Message at the Leadership Summit, Willow Creek, August, 1999.

Cymbala, James. Interview by Carl Johnson, 24 August, 2007. Brooklyn, NY.

Ireland, David. "Minority Perspectives of Interracial Relationships in Large Multiracial Churches," Ph.D. diss., Regent University, 2000.

Johnson, Diana. "Concept Mapping of Supervisor Competence: A Comparative Analysis of Expert and Novice Supervisors," Ph.D. diss., Fordham University, 2007.

Mathews, Tony. "Equipping Staff and Lay Leaders to Intentionally Grow, Nurture and Lead a Multicultural Congregation," D.Min. project, Southwest Baptist Theological Seminary, 2000.

Nicole, Roger. Lectures on Systematic Theology at Gordon-Conwell Theological Seminary, S. Hamilton, MA, Spring 1973.

Samples, T. A. "An Ethical Analysis of Multiethnic Congregations in Los Angeles," Ph.D. diss., University of Southern California, 1997.

VITA

C arl Johnson has been pastor of Gracepoint Gospel Fellowship in New City, New York for over thirty-three years. He has seen the church grow from an attendance of about 140 in 1977 to an average of 1200 to 1400 weekly in three services in 2011. During this time the makeup of the congregation has changed dramatically moving from a completely white church to one that now boasts over 70 different ethnicities with almost equal numbers of whites, blacks and Hispanics and a smaller percentage of Asians.

Carl received a Bachelor of Science degree with a major in Mathematics and a minor in Physics from Oral Roberts University in 1971. He holds a Master of Divinity degree from Gordon-Conwell Theological Seminary in South Hamilton, Massachusetts and a Doctor of Ministry degree from the Kings Seminary in Van Nuys, California. Carl and his wife Sherry, who holds a doctorate in Counseling Psychology from Fordham University, have often traveled together to various mission fields to teach in Bible school settings and in seminars and pastors conferences. They are parents of three children and grandparents of five.

Their travel has taken them to Bible schools in Poland, India, Argentina and Tanzania, and to pastors' seminars in Colombia and India. Carl has served on the boards of the Warsaw Theological Seminary, Seminario Biblico de Fe in Buenos Aires, as well as Concerts of Prayer Greater New York. He has arranged for extension courses at Gracepoint Gospel through Christian Life College of Chicago and is active in teaching many of those classes and mentoring students toward ministry.

ENDNOTES

Chapter 1

[1] David Ireland, What Color is Your God? (Verona, NJ: Impact Publishing, 2000), 85; (How Pastors See Ministry in America, Barna Research Group, Glendale, CA, 1990 survey).

[2] George Yancey, One Body, One Spirit: Principles for Multiracial Churches (Downers Grove, IL: InterVarsity Publishing, 2003), 14. Yancey prefers the term "multiracial church" since he is convinced that the major barrier for churches to overcome is in the mingling of races, not simply ethnicities. This is obvious if one considers that in any given white, black or Hispanic church there are often several ethnicities represented.

[3] Donald A. McGavran, Understanding Church Growth (Grand Rapids: Eerdmans Publishing, 1980), 62.

[4] Ibid.

[5] Douglas W. Ruffle, "Building Blocks for a Multicultural Congregation," Quarterly Review 13 (Fall 1993): 74.

[6] Ibid.

[7] Henry S. Wilson, "Multicultural Christian Community: A Bouquet of Multicultural Flowers," Word and World 24, no. 2 (Spring 2004): 174.

[8] Kathy Black, Culturally Conscious Worship (St. Louis: Chalice Press, 2000), 15. Figures are taken from the United States Bureau of Census Web site.

[9] David A. Anderson, Multicultural Ministry: Finding Your Church's Unique Rhythm (Grand Rapids: Zondervan, 2004), 40.

[10] Ken Uyeda Fong, Pursuing the Pearl: A Comprehensive Resource for Multi-Asian Ministry (Valley Forge, PA: Judson Press, 1999), 230.

[11] Dinesh D'Souza, The End of Racism: Principles for a Multiracial Society (New York: Simon and Schuster, 1996), 11.

[12] Silla Brush, "The New Shape of the Nation," U.S. News and World Report, 2 October 2006, 46.

[13] Arthur M. Schlesinger, Jr., The Disuniting of America: Reflections on a Multicultural Society (New York: W. W. Norton, 1991), 10.

[14] James and Lillian Breckenridge, What Color is Your God? Multicultural Education in the Church (Wheaton, IL: Victor Books, 1984), 40.

[15] "All the World Comes to Queens," National Geographic (September 1998).

[16] Roger Sanjek, The Future of Us All (Ithaca, NY: Cornell Univ. Press, 1998), 1, 395 n. 1.

[17] Ray A. Bakke, A Theology As Big As the City (Downers Grove, IL: InterVarsity Press, 1997), 12-13.

[18] New People–New Cultures, Ramapo College newsletter, Spring 2002, 4.

[19] Toinette M. Eugene, "Multicultural Ministry: Theory, Practice, Theology," Chicago Theological Seminary Register 84, no. 2 (Spring 1994): 1.

[20] McGavran, 62.

[21] C. Peter Wagner, Our Kind of People: The Ethical Dimensions of Church Growth in America (Atlanta: John Knox Press, 1979), 1.

[22] C. Peter Wagner, Strategies for Church Growth (Ventura, CA: Regal Books, 1987), 191.

[23] Ibid.

[24] Ibid.

[25] Black, 15.

[26] Wilson, 178.

[27] Ibid.

Chapter 2

[28] Hines and DeYoung, 3.

[29] Black, 35.

[30] Curtiss DeYoung and others, United by Faith: The Multicultural Congregation as an Answer to the Problem of Race (New York: Oxford University Press, 2003), 149.

[31] Ibid.

[32] David Ireland, What Color is Your God? 65.

[33] George E. Ladd, A Theology of the New Testament (Grand Rapids, MI: Eerdmans Publishing, 1993), 66-67.

[34] Julius Scott, The Gospel in Black & White: Theological Resources for Racial Reconciliation, Dennis L. Okholm, ed., (Downers Grove, IL: InterVarsity Press, 1998), 132.

[35] Wayne Grudem, Systematic Theology: An Introduction to Biblical Doctrine (Grand Rapids: Zondervan Publishing, 1994), 256.

[36] Ibid., 257.

[37] Larry Crabb, When the Leader Gets in the Way, Message at the Leadership Summit, Willow Creek, 1999.

[38] Millard J. Erickson, Introducing Christian Doctrine (Grand Rapids: Baker Academic, 2001), 112.

[39] Ibid.

[40] Ibid.

[41] Scott, 133

[42] Ibid.

[43] Ibid.

[44] Ibid., 133. Legalistic Christians today still have the tendency to be absorbed with food and drink. They can easily miss the primary message of this passage - that is the reconciliation of men.

[45] C. F. Keil and F. Delitzsch, Biblical Commentary on the Old Testament (Grand Rapids: Eerdmans Publishing, 1971), 344.

[46] Ibid.

[47] Ibid.

[48] Okholm, 132.

[49] Ibid., 134.

[50] F. F. Bruce, The Epistle to the Galations: A Commentary on the Greek Text, New International Greek Testament Commentary (Grand Rapids: Eerdmans Publishing, 1982), 188.

[51] Ibid., 187.

[52] Ibid.

[53] Ibid., 189.

[54] Okholm, 132.

[55] Ibid., 135.

[56] This entire passage (1 Corinthians 1:10 to 4:21) deals with the problem of division in the church. Paul makes it clear that disunity arises out of improper allegiances to men which imply that men have something to do with salvation. Paul begins his corrective word with reference to the cross of Christ. He ultimately is proposing that division and discrimination are a contradiction of the message of the cross which is salvation through Christ and Christ alone.

[57] Okholm, 135.

[58] Ibid., 136.

[59] Ibid., 139.

[60] Erickson, 172.

[61] Grudem, 442.

[62] Ibid., 449.

[63] Erickson, 173.

[64] Ibid.

[65] Ibid.

[66] Ibid.

[67] Ibid., 176.

[68] Ibid.

[69] Ibid.

[70] Ibid.

[71] Ibid.

[72] Ibid., 177.

[73] Wagner, Our Kind of People, 104/

[74] Ibid.

[75] Ibid.

[76] Ken Hamm, Carl Wieland, and Don Batten, One Blood: The Biblical Answer to Racism (Green Forest, AR: Master Books, 2000), 54.

[77] Ibid., 55.

[78] John Ornguze, Heaven – for Whites Only (El Cajon, CA: Christian Service Publishers, 2000), 22.

[79] Clara La Plante, Who Benefits from Reconciliation? The Christian Ministry, May-June 1995, 20-22.

[80] Ireland, What Color is Your God? 68.

[81] Ibid.

[82] Jerome, Homolies 21, FC 48:170, in Andrew Louth Genesis 1-11: Ancient Christian Commentary on Scripture (Downers Grove, Il.: Inter-Varsity, 2001), 169.

[83] John Chrysostom, Homolies on Genesis 30.13, FC 82:229, in Louth, Genesis 1-11, 168-9.

[84] Faye Flam, "DNA shows links between all living humans," Journal News (16 April 2001), 3E.

[85]

[86] Ibid.

[87] Ibid. If it were possible to eliminate the word "race" and the commonly held view of race from our vocabulary then one would also be eliminating the word and concept of "racism." This would obviously be problematic since sin has caused feelings of pride and superiority and along with those a natural disdain and intolerance for people of other colors, customs and physical characteristics than oneself. "Racial" discrimination must be addressed and thus the need for language to do so. Clarifying the notion of race should be a goal of theological education as one teaches the doctrine of man and addresses the vital concept of the "image of God."

[88] Ireland, What Color is Your God? 70.

[89] Ibid., 71.

[90] Ibid.

[91] Ibid., 73.

[92] Ibid.

[93] Ibid., 76.

[94] Ibid., 21.

[95] Albert Pero, "Ministry in Multi-cultural Church." Currents in Theology and Mission 17 (Fall 1990): 68.

[96] Ireland, What Color is Your God? 76.

[97] DeYoung et al., 12.

[98] Norman Anthony Peart, Separate No More: Understanding and Developing Racial Reconciliation in Your Church (Grand Rapids: Baker Books, 2000), 116.

[99] Ibid.

[100] Wilson, 175.

[101] Elizabeth Conde-Frazier, S. Steve King, and Gary Parrett. A Many Colored Kingdom: Multicultural Dynamics for Spiritual Formation (Grand Rapids: Baker Academics, 2005), 170.Ibid.

[102] Ibid.

[103] Peart, 117.

[104] DeYoung, et al., 14.

[105] Ibid.

[106] Ibid., 15.

[107] Ibid.

[108] Pero, 68.

[109] Peart, 118.

[110] Ibid.

[111] Ibid.

[112] DeYoung et al., 16.

[113] Ibid., 17.

[114] Ibid., 18.

[115] William Willimon, "Everyone Whom the Lord Our God Calls: Acts 2 and the Miracle of Pentecost Preaching in a Multicultural Context," Journal for Preachers 25, no. 4 (Pentecost 2002): 4.

[116] Ibid., 119.

[117] Roger Nicole, Lectures on Systematic Theology at Gordon-Conwell Theological Seminary, S. Hamilton, MA: Spring, 1973.

[118] Verlyn Verbrugge, New International Dictionary of New Testament Theology: Abridged Edition (Grand Rapids, MI: Zondervan Publishing, 2000), 293.

[119] Lawrence O. Richards, Expository Dictionary of Bible Words (Grand Rapids: Regency, 1985), 514.

[120] Verbrugge, 293.

[121] Bauer, 38.

[122] Verbrugge, 293.

[123] Richards, 514.

[124] Ibid.

[125] Hines and DeYoung, 3.

[126] Verbrugge, 293.

[127] Richards, 515.

[128] Verbrugge, 293.

[129] Hines and DeYoung, 3.

[130] Richards, 515.

[131] Verbrugge, 293.

[132] Ibid.

[133] Ibid.

[134] C. K. Barrett, The Second Epistle to the Corinthians (New York: Harper and Row, 1973), 163.

[135] Barrett, 170.

[136] Philip Hughes, The Second Epistle to the Corinthians (Grand Rapids: Eerdmans Publishing, 1962), 197.

[137] Barrett, 171.

138 Hughes, 199.
139 Barrett, 170.
140 Hughes, 199.
141 Barrett, 172.
142 Hines and DeYoung, 3.
143 Hughes, 197.
144 Ibid., 198.
145 Peart, 112-113.
146 Ibid., 294.
147 Walter Elwell and Robert Yarbrough, Encountering the New Testament, (Grand Rapids: Baker Academics, 2005), 245.
148 Richards, 515.
149 Hines, 3.
150 Peart, 119.
151 Ibid., 120.
152 Ibid.
153 DeYoung, 22.
154 Ibid., 23.
155 Ibid., 24.
156 Peart, 121.
157 Ibid., 122.
158 Ibid., 124.
159 DeYoung et al., 26.
160 Ibid.
161 Ibid., 27.
162 Ibid., 29.
163 Ibid.
164 Ibid., 35.
165 Stephen Mott, "Multicultural Inclusiveness in Revelation," Christian Social Action (June 1993), 37.
166 Ibid.
167 Peart, 124.
168 Ibid.
169 Robin Gill, A Textbook of Christian Ethics (Edinburgh: T. & T. Clark, 1985), 528.
170 Jay Adams, The Time is at Hand (Nutley, NJ: Presbyterian and Reformed Publishing, 1970), 3.
171 Law, 3.
172 Ibid., 3-4.
173 Ibid., 10.
174 Ibid.

[175] Andrew Sung Park, Racial Conflict and Healing: An Asian-American Theological Perspective (Maryknoll, NY: Orbis Books, 1996), 67.

[176] Ibid.

[177] Ibid.

[178] Ibid.

[179] Ibid., 70.

[180] Ibid.

[181] Ibid., 73.

[182] Mott, 37.

[183] Blount and Tisdale, 16.

[184] Ibid.

[185] Ibid., 17.

[186] Ibid.

[187] Ibid.

[188] Ibid.

[189] Ibid.

[190] Ibid.

[191] Ibid., 18.

[192] Ibid.

[193] Ibid.

[194] Ibid., 19.

[195] Ibid.

[196] Ibid.

[197] Ibid.

[198] Ibid., 20.

[199] Ibid., 21.

[200] Ibid.

[201] Ibid.

[202] Ibid.

[203] Ibid.

[204] Ibid.

[205] Ibid.

[206] Ibid., 22.

[207] Ibid.

Chapter 3

[1] Stephen Rhodes, Where the Nations Meet: The Church in a Multicultural World (Downers Grove, IL: InterVarsity Press, 1998), 13-14.

[2] Michael Hawn, One Bread, One Body: Exploring Cultural Diversity in Worship (Bethesda, MD: The Alban Institute, 2003), 35.

[3] Anderson, 9.

[4] Charles Foster, Embracing Diversity: Leadership in Multicultural Congregations (Bethesda, MD: The Alban Institute, 1997), 1.

[5] Wagner, Our Kind of People, 28.

[6] Foster, 9.

[7] Anderson, 10.

[8] Ibid., 21.

[9] Ibid.

[10] Joseph R. Jeter Jr. and Ronald J. Allen, One Gospel, Many Ears: Preaching for Different Listeners in the Congregation (St. Louis: Chalice Press, 2002), 108.

[11] Ibid. Some would include "unconditional love" and a "stand against common oppression" as contributing factors in a church that is welcoming a gay and lesbian population. A number of authors include sexual orientation as an element of the diversity that God is pleased with. This author sees the Biblical ideal as an environment that is accepting and loving of all but loving enough to confront behavior that is offensive to God and contrary to His directives and ultimately damaging to the individual (Lev. 18:22; Romans 1:27; 1 Cor. 6:9). Paul and his Jewish contemporaries did not distinguish between lawful and illicit homosexuality as many do today. For the inspired author this sexual preference was by nature wrong in any context.

[12] Jeter, 108.

[13] Wagner, Our Kind of People, 12.

[14] Glen H. Stassen and David P. Gushee, Kingdom Ethics: Following Jesus in Contemporary Context (Downers Grove, IL: InterVarsity Press, 2003), 390.

[15] Anderson, 19. The idea of bookends is illustrated by the voting patterns of whites and blacks in the 2000 Presidential elections. Only 8% of blacks (61% of whom identified themselves as born-again) voted for the self-identified (white) evangelical candi-

date, George Bush. No group protested the legitimacy of Bush's election more strongly.

[16] Ibid.

[17] Ibid.

[18] McGavran, 198.

[19] Wagner, Our Kind of People, 1.

[20] Ibid., 4.

[21] Yancey, One Body, One Spirit, 30.

[22] Wagner, Our Kind of People, 6.

[23] Ibid., 8.

[24] Ibid., 9.

[25] Ibid.

[26] McGavran, 198.

[27] Yancey, One Body, One Spirit, 30-31.

[28] Wagner, Our Kind of People, 11.

[29] Ibid.

[30] Ibid.

[31] Ibid.

[32] Ibid.

[33] Ibid., 16.

[34] Ibid.

[35] Ibid.

[36] Ibid.

[37] Ibid.

[38] Ibid.

[39] Yancey, One Body, One Spirit, 31. Assimilation is an oft used word in the church. It is important that assimilation be concerned with enfolding people into the life and ministry of the church but that it not mean the surrender of the individual's or the group's cultural uniqueness.

[40] Andres Tapia, "The Myth of Racial Progress," Christianity Today 37 (October 1993): 18.

[41] Wilson, 180.

[42] Jürgen Moltmann, "Political Theology," Theology Today 27 (1971), 22.

[43] Ibid. Moltmann looks forward to a future made up of a new humanity - a humanity free from racism, injustice, captivity, oppression, prejudice, war, and hate. He interprets the past as being characterized by a pluralism of cultures, nations, religions, and churches, which he regards as evil. His theology of hope embraces a future of the "singular": in order to avoid possible extinction, all

peoples must participate in one new community, which Moltmann predicts will erase cultural distinctives, racial barriers, and social classes. Moltmann concludes that churches that continue to be distinct from others are churches of the past. The churches of the future, those that fully participate in the dynamics of Christian hope, will overcome human differences and make the plural singular. This is, of course, exactly what Wagner argues should not take place – the losing of each group's cultural identity.

[44] John R. W. Stott, Our Guilty Silence (Grand Rapids: Eerdmans Publishing, 1967), 71.

[45] Ibid.

[46] Wagner, Our Kind of People, 19.

[47] Ibid.

[48] Ibid., 22.

[49] Ibid., 26.

[50] Ibid., 23

[51] Ibid.

[52] Ibid., 24.

[53] Ibid.

[54] Vinson Synan, The Century of the Holy Spirit:100 Years of Pentecostal and Charismatic Renewal (Nashville: Thomas Nelson Publishers, 2001), 125.

[55] Randy Woodley, Living in Color: Embracing God's Passion for Ethnic Diversity (Downers Grove, IL: InterVarsity Press, 2001), 98.

[56] Ibid.

[57] Ibid., 25.

[58] Wilson, 177.

[59] Yancey, One Body, One Spirit, 36.

[60] Ibid., 37.

[61] Manuel Ortiz, One New People: Models for Developing a Multicultural Church, (Downers Grove, IL: InterVarsity Press, 1996), 13.

[62] Foster, 2.

[63] Jeter, 109.

[64] Yancey, One Body, One Spirit, 48.

[65] Lane, 171. This researcher has experienced a deep sense of gratitude and appreciation from minorities when one is willing to address the topic of racism in a message and acknowledge the failure of the white church to reach out to and minister to the needs of minorities.

[66] Ibid.

[67] Wilson, 173.

[68] Hawn, 6.

[69] Ibid., 11.

[70] Eric H. F. Law, Inclusion: Making Room for Grace (St. Louis: Chalice Press, 2000), 42.

[71] Wilson, 181.

[72] Hawn, 12.

[73] Yancey, One Body, One Spirit, 41.

[74] Ibid., 110.

[75] Wilson, 173.

[76] Lane, 23.

[77] Joel L. Swerdlow, "Global Culture," National Geographic 196:2 (August 1999): 3.

[78] Foster, xiii.

[79] Ibid., 14

[80] Ibid.

[81] Lane, 27.

[82] Ibid.

[83] Ibid., 30.

[84] Ibid., 37.

[85] Ibid.

[86] Jeter, 111.

[87] James Cymbala, interview by Carl Johnson, August 24, 2007, Brooklyn, NY.

[88] Peart, 180.

[89] Yancey, One Body, One Spirit, 66. Yancey,

[90] Hawn, 80.

[91] Ibid., 85.

[92] Ibid.

[93] Ibid., 94.

[94] Ibid., 47.

[95] Ibid., 50.

[96] Wilson, 179.

[97] Yancey, One Body, One Spirit, 109-110.

[98] Raleigh Washington, and Glen Kehrein, Break Down the Walls, Experiencing Biblical Reconciliation and Unity in the Body of Christ. Chicago: Moody Press, 1997 127.

[99] Yancey, One Body, One Spirit, 111.

[100] Ibid., 113.

[101] George Yancey, Beyond Black and White: Reflections on Racial Reconciliation (Grand Rapids: Baker Books, 1996), 11.

[102] Yancey, One Body, One Spirit, 73.

[103] Hawn, 113.

[104] Ibid., 117.

[105] Ibid., 121.

[106] Ibid., 122.

[107] Ibid., 125.

[108] Ibid., 81.

[109] Kenneth Barker, ed., The New International Study Bible (Grand Rapids: Zondervan Publishing House, 1995), 1656.

[110] Peart, 146.

[111] Yancey, One Body, One Spirit, 86.

[112] Ibid., 93.

[113] Ibid., 101.

[114] Ibid., 106.

[115] Ibid. 114.

[116] Ibid., 120.

[117] Ibid., 122.

[118] Spencer Perkins and Chris Rice, More Than Equals (Downers Grove, IL: InterVarsity Press, 1993), 132.

[119] Ibid., 139.

[120] Hawn, 5.

[121] Ibid., 6.

[122] Ibid., 7.

[123] Ibid.

[124] Ibid.

[125] Black, 19.

[126] Ibid., 8.

[127] Ibid.

[128] Ibid., 8-9.

[129] Ibid., 13.

[130] Ibid., 16.

[131] Ibid., 17.

[132] Ibid.

[133] The application of this idea may be extremely controversial as one considers, for example, the role of women and the idea of Biblical headship as that is contrasted with cultural views of women's roles and of headship. Often cultural views may be read into Scripture rather than letting Scripture speak for itself.

[134] Ibid., 18.

[136] Ibid.
[137] Ibid., 19.
[138] Ibid.
[139] Lane, 171.
[140] Ibid., 17.
[141] Ibid., 20-21.
[142] Ibid., 32.
[143] Ibid., 48-49.
[144] Lane, 66.
[145] Ibid., 73.
[146] Hawn, 25.
[147] Ibid.
[148] Lane, 86–87.
[149] Ibid., 94.
[150] Ibid., 98.
[151] Ibid., 103.
[152] Hawn, 21.
[153] Lane, 110.
[154] Ibid., 112, 114.
[155] Ibid.
[156] Lane, 117.
[157] Ibid.
[158] Hawn, 23
[159] Ibid., 24
[160] Ibid.
[161] Peart, 130.
[162] Ibid., 134.
[163] Ibid., 135-136.
[164] Ibid., 137.
[165] Ibid.
[166] Ibid.
[167] Ibid., 138.
[168] Ibid., 139.
[169] Ibid., 140.
[170] Stassen, 390.
[171] Peart, 140.
[172] Ibid.
[173] David Ireland, "Minority Perspectives of Interracial Relationships," 5.
[174] Foster, 3.
[175] Eugene, 5.

[176] Wilson, 177.

[177] Black, 21.

[178] Conde-Frazier, et. al 171.

[179] Foster, 10.

[180] Ibid., 12.

[181] Rupert Lloyd, "Managing a Multicultural Congregation," Leadership 1 (Winter 1990): 36.

[182] Ibid., 37-38.

[183] Ibid., 38.

[184] Ibid.

[185] Ibid., 37.

[186] David Ireland, "Minority Perspectives of Interracial Relationships," 5.

[187] John Maxwell, Developing the Leaders Around You (Nashville: Thomas Nelson, 1995), 17.

[188] David Ireland, "Minority Perspectives of Interracial Relationships," 5.

[189] Ibid.

[190] Peart, 144.

[191] Ibid., 147. Eugene says, "Three things provide a focus for a minister becoming better prepared for multicultural ministry." The first is language. The learning of the minority language is indispensable, he says, for multicultural ministry, not only for better communication, but to appreciate the identity of the community. Second, being able to situate where a culture group is in the adaptation process can help shape pastoral strategies. And third, he suggests, communicative competence – the capacity to understand the communication pathways of a culture – requires knowing how the culture communicates and how it feels in the presence of other cultures.

[192] Ibid., 14.8.

[193] Greer Anne Ng. "One Faith, One Baptism – One Liturgy? Worship in a Multicultural, Multifaith Context," Reformed Liturgy & Music 30 no 3, 146-149.

[194] Ibid.

[195] Ibid.

[196] Barbara Wilkerson, Goals of Multicultural Religious Education (Birmingham, AL: Religious Education Press, 1997), 22.

[197] Peart, 87.

[198] Wilkerson, 22.

[199] Ellen Renee Dill, "Unity and Difference in the Multicultural Congregation," The Christian Ministry, May-June 1995, 25.

[200] Wilkerson, 22.

[201] Ibid., 18.

[202] Ray Bakke and Jim Hart, The Urban Christian: Effective Ministry in Today's Urban World (Downers Grove, IL: InterVarsity Press, 1987).

[203] Ibid., 12.

[204] Wilson, 180.

[205] W. E. Whalley, "The Inner City Church in a Multicultural Environment," The Baptist Quarterly 33, (Jan 1989): 48.

[206] Peart, 105.

[207] Ibid.

[208] Ibid., 107.

[209] Ibid., 114-115.

[210] Okholm, ed., 14.

[211] Ibid.

[212] Perkins and Rice, 167.

[213] Ibid., 15.

[214] Ibid., 17.

[215] Ibid.

[216] Ibid., 18.

[217] Ibid., 20.

[218] Ibid., 21.

[219] Ibid., 23.

[220] Ibid., 28.

[221] Ibid., 30.

[222] Ibid.

[223] Willimon, 5.

[224] Ibid., 4.

[225] Ibid.

[226] Ibid., 5.

[227] Ibid., 6.

[228] Ibid. 8.

[229] Ibid.

[230] Ibid., 7.

[231] Ibid., 9.

Chapter 4

[232] Yancey, One Body, One Spirit, 67-69.

[233] Ibid., 163.

[234] Ibid., 167.

[235] Ibid., 55-59.

[236] Ibid., 60.

[237] Ibid., 126.

[238] Ibid., 100-101.

[239] Ibid., 101.

[240] Ibid., 104.

[241] Ibid., 109.

[242] Ibid., 86.

[243] Ibid., 87.

[244] Ibid.

[246] Ibid., 69.

[247] Ibid., 140.

Appendix B

[1] Maria Darcy, Debbiesiu Lee, and Terence J. G. Tracey, "Complementary Approaches to Individual Differences Using Paired Comparisons and Multidimensional Scaling: Applications to Multicultural Counseling Competence," Journal of Counseling Psychology, Vol. 51, no. 2, (2004) 139.

[2] William R. Myers, Research in Ministry: A Primer for the Doctor of Ministry Program (Chicago: Exploration Press, 1993), 25. Myers says such research often results in the presentation of a narrative in which the persons involved experience the process of transformation. The pro-active researcher, therefore, intentionally and actively engages in the experience that is being researched. On the face of it, this third research method – the pro-active – is radically different from methods one and two and sounds congruent with those implications of transformation most closely associated with Judeo-Christian conceptions of ministry. It more clearly fits, for example, the theological claims made by most Doctor of Ministry programs.

[3] Mark J. Cartledge, Practical Theology: Charismatic and Empirical Perspectives (Carlisle, Cumbria, UK: Paternoster Press, 2003), 81.

[4] Andrew Gol and Stephen Cook, "Exploring the Underlying Dimensions of Coping: A Concept Mapping Approach," Journal of Social and Clinical Psychology 23, no. 2, (2004): 157.

[5] Samuel Jackson Buser, "A Counseling Practitioner's Primer to the Use of Multidimensional Scaling," Journal of Counseling and Development 67, (March 1989): 420.

[6] Diana Johnson, "Concept Mapping of Supervisor Competence: A Comparative Analysis of Expert and Novice Supervisors," Doctoral Dissertation, Fordham University, (2007), 39.

[7] Fred Borgen and David Barnett, "Applying Cluster Analysis in Counseling Psychology Research," Journal of Counseling Psychology 34, no. 4, (1987), 20.

[8] Barbara Paulson, Derek Truscott, and Janice Stuart, "Clients Perceptions of Helpful Experiences in Counseling," Journal of Counseling Psychology 46, no. 3 (1999): 318.

[9] Johnson, 38.

[10] Ibid., 37-38.

[11] Borgen and Barnett, 461.

[12] Ibid.

[13] Buser, 420.

[14] Louis F. Fitzgerald and Lawrence J. Hubert, "Multidimensional Scaling: Some Possibilities for Counseling Psychology," Journal of Counseling Psychology 34, no. 4, (1987): 469.

[15] M. L. Davison, P. S. Richards, and J. B. Rounds, "Multidimensional Scaling in Counseling Research and Practice," Journal of Counseling and Development 65, (1986): 178.

[16] Johnson, 39.

[17] Gol and Cook, 155.

[18] Borgen and Barnett, 138.

[19] Paulson, Truscott, and Stuart, 318.

[20] Gol and Cook, 158.

[21] Johnson, 57.

[22] Leedy, 164.